The Art of
Bonsai
DESIGN

The Art of
Bonsai
DESIGN

Colin Lewis

STERLING PUBLISHING CO., INC.
New York

Library of Congress Cataloging-in-Publication Data

Lewis, Colin.
    The art of bonsai design / Colin Lewis.
        p. cm.
    Includes index.
    ISBN 0-4027-0070-9
       1. Bonsai. I. Title.
    SB433.5 L473 2001
    635.9'772—dc21   00-53196

1 3 5 7 9 10 8 6 4 2

First paperback edition published in 2002 by
Sterling Publishing Company, Inc.
387 Park Avenue South, New York, N.Y. 10016
© 2001 by Colin Lewis
Distributed in Canada by Sterling Publishing
c/o Canadian Manda Group, One Atlantic Avenue, Suite 105
Toronto, Ontario, Canada M6K 3E7
Distributed in Australia by Capricorn Link (Australia) Pty. Ltd.
P.O. Box 704, Windsor, NSW 2756 Australia

Printed in China
All rights reserved

Sterling ISBN 0-8069-7137-1 Hardcover
ISBN 1-4027-0070-9 Paperback

Contents

Foreword

In memory of my father,
who showed me how
to plant potatoes

However you care to look at it, bonsai is an entirely unique phenomenon, riddled with contradictions and frustrations. Lost somewhere in the no-man's-land between art and horticulture, it attracts enthusiasts from both disciplines, yet it gains full recognition from neither. For instance, bonsai is undoubtedly an art form; but this book, and all others on the subject, is displayed in the gardening section of your bookstore. On the other hand, in spite of the fact that bonsai demands an intensely intimate involvement with horticulture, often coaxing trees to perform the most surprising tricks, by and large the horticultural establishment regards the practice as frivolous and somewhat lacking in dignity.

Newcomers to bonsai struggle with both the horticultural and the aesthetic aspects. Although the former can be learned relatively easily from general gardening books as well as the multitude of specialist bonsai publications, local clubs and even the Internet, the aesthetic skills and sensitivities are rather harder to acquire. This problem is made even more frustrating by the fact that the trees that are displayed on your benches today are largely the product of your skill level several—sometimes many—years ago. When you embark on a bonsai project, whether you're brimming with confidence or tortured by self-doubt, the one thing you know for sure is that this is just the beginning of a long, magical journey.

Many newcomers lose heart at the first failure, or when they see wonderful mature bonsai specimens for the first time, believing that the ability to create such images is far beyond them. They're not wrong—it does take time and dedication to achieve such results—but even the most talented and successful bonsai artists were beginners once, making precisely the same mistakes and wrestling with exactly the same uncertainties.

I am no exception. When I first decided to write this book, I considered calling it *A Catalog of Errors*—for that is largely what it is. Making mistakes, realizing that they have been made and then devising ways of rectifying them is part of the bonsai learning process. It has taught me more than simply how to grow attractive bonsai; it has altered my entire outlook on life. When I look at the photographs of the progress of my trees, I blush when I recall how proud I felt of the images that now seem so ridiculous to me. But I'm not ashamed of my earlier naïveté, nor of the many mistakes I have made along the way. They are all revealed in this book, along with the lessons they have taught me and some of the more recent work I have done that capitalizes on those lessons.

If you're a relative newcomer to bonsai, by reading this book you'll be able to learn from my mistakes and find hope and encouragement from the knowledge that even the most bizarre first attempts can eventually become fine bonsai that you can justifiably be proud of.

If you're a more experienced bonsai artist you're permitted to snigger a little as you first flip through these pages—but not for long. Here you'll find many of the missing pieces of the jigsaw puzzle that you have been slowly completing over the years. You'll discover new ideas and, hopefully, the inspiration and courage to progress *your* art the way *you* want to (and brave the taunts of your peers along the way!). You'll also encounter comments and suggestions that will prompt you to re-examine your own thoughts. Or some that might inspire you to take greater strides towards freeing bonsai from the chains of tradition and the stigma of "ornamental gardening," and establish it in its rightful place as an art form—with all the creative potential and dignity of any other.

Colin Lewis, June 2000

Introduction

Bonsai as a Western art

ARE WE DENYING OUR OWN CULTURAL HERITAGE IN OUR PURSUIT OF JAPANESE STYLE?

Although Japanese and Western cultures are worlds apart, a number of comparisons can be made.

IT DOESN'T really matter whether our individual fascination with bonsai began via gardening, art or a general interest in things Eastern, we all have much to learn. Those who were introduced to bonsai through gardening will have knowledge and confidence that will give them a head start in the horticultural processes involved. Those who came to bonsai from an artistic background will already have a grasp of the aesthetic principles of line, form, balance, and so on. Those whose bonsai activities began with a general interest in Japanese art and culture are likely to be able to understand the philosophical requirements of this demanding discipline.

However, those in the latter group are in the greatest danger of making a fundamental mistake: that of trying to copy the Japanese rather than learning from them. The difference may be subtle, but it is very significant. The Japanese have built up their wealth of knowledge over centuries, so we rightly turn to them for practical horticultural and artistic guidance. In this way we have the advantage of being able to become reasonably proficient in a relatively short time. But it is important not to lose sight of our own cultural and environmental heritage when designing our bonsai.

A major turning point in my bonsai thinking occurred when I heard John Yoshio Naka say: "Don't try to make your tree look like a bonsai—try to make your bonsai look like a tree." At first this seems like an obvious piece of advice. But how often do you hear novices talk about "Japanese shapes" or display their trees amidst an eclectic clutter of Eastern paraphernalia?

Whether your personal preference is for lifelike representations of lowland specimens, rugged mountain trees or almost abstract living sculptures—in the final analysis we are all trying to reach a similar goal: to create an aesthetically pleasing, more or less treelike image. But what qualifies as "treelike" depends very much on an individual's cultural and environmental background.

Although Japanese and Western cultures are worlds apart, a number of comparisons can be made, particularly in the way artists have traditionally depicted trees two-dimensionally. Inevitably, this has had a profound impact on our mental images of the "fantasy" trees we are trying to create—in both cultures.

Japan had no master landscape painters such as Constable or Vermeer. In fact individual, one-of-a-kind paintings were rare. The majority of Japanese pictures were narrative prints illustrating a story or legend, often reproduced in large numbers from woodcuts, where the image stands in relief on the side grain. The lack of perspective and tonal range in Japanese woodcuts may, in part, explain why a bonsai has a "front" and is not a truly three-dimensional work of art. To find a historical Western equivalent we must look at artists such as Gustave Doré and Thomas Bewick, whose illustrations were also reproduced in print form, but from wood engravings where the image is cut into the end grain of the wood. The far more intricate line work that could be introduced in wood engravings meant that their images of trees contained far more depth and texture, although only in black and white.

9

The print above (c.1825) is typically Japanese, yet its artist depicted the maple foliage on the right of the picture in precisely the same way that Bewick handled the oak foliage on the overhanging branch on the wood engraving on the right. Both artists worked with a similar medium at a similar time, but in vastly different cultures.

Something about trees touches the soul; trees evoke childhood memories of sights, sounds and smells.

A major influence on the Japanese woodcut artists' depiction of trees was the fact that art and calligraphy were inextricably linked. Woodcut artists were influenced by the fluid, single-brush-stroke trunk lines and vague hints of foliage. A few bold lines and simple areas of color can tell us all there is to know. This simplified approach to art was reinforced by the minimalist teachings of Zen Buddhism, which pervades all aspects of Japanese culture. It is easy to see how this has influenced the Japanese approach to bonsai.

On the other hand, the wood engravers in the West were influenced by the landscape painters' quest for realism and detail and, indeed, the public demanded it. Since the use of color was uneconomical and impractical, they developed techniques using light, shade and intricate detail to achieve this end. As a result, their illustrations were heavy, somber and rather intense.

Moving forward to this century, we can find a more direct comparison between Western and Japanese depiction of trees. The same use of simple line, flat areas of color and distillation of form of the Japanese print became necessary in the West with the development of cartoon animation. To be visually (and economically) successful in cartoon form, images of trees have to be simplified, carefully analyzed and broken down to their basic elements. Only the bare essentials are retained, just enough to describe the tree. These elements are presented in a way that also evokes the character and spirit of the tree and sets the mood of the scene. Isn't this exactly what we try to do with our bonsai design, albeit in three dimensions and with a more complex medium?

If you look carefully at the way trees of both familiar and unfamiliar species are drawn in Walt Disney films such as *Jungle Book*, you will see some startling comparisons with Japanese woodcut prints. In fact, the early animators learned much from studying the Japanese artists' techniques, but did not copy their style because their culture, subject matter and audience were entirely different.

Once we recognize the common aims, problems and solutions between the Japanese two-dimensional artist and the Japanese bonsai artist, it's easy to acknowledge a parallel relationship between the Western bonsai artist and the cartoon animator. And since we are Westerners—and our vision of trees is influenced by Western environmental and cultural factors—it could be argued that we have as much to learn about simplified images of trees from Walt Disney's animators as from the Japanese artists.

The point of this culture-shock treatment is to bring bonsai another step Westward. There are still taboos and superstitions in many aspects of Japanese society, including bonsai. If bonsai is an art form, it must, to some extent, be self-expressive. What we want to express about trees and our emotional response toward them must, surely, be rooted in our culture.

I am not suggesting that we all turn to Donald Duck for inspiration, but for some guidance on how to produce credible, emotive, highly simplified images of trees, you may find it more useful to refer to some of the better-animated cartoons than spend precious time and effort trying to negotiate your way around the distractions of the cultural, philosophical and artistic differences that exist between us and the Japanese. If we try to copy the Japanese and attempt to produce "Japanese shapes" or "Japanese-looking" bonsai, we will more than likely be frustrated.

Our trees, our heritage

There is much talk about developing a Western style, or even British or American styles, of bonsai. In order to begin any such task we must recognize that our natural environment is an enormous influence on who we are, and must understand why we are so obsessed with creating bonsai. Surely, before we can begin to develop our own style we must filter out all those bonsai teachings that are uniquely cultural, or even philosophical, and replace them with our own. Inevitably we will continue to be heavily influenced by Japanese bonsai artists, but we must learn that it is not a sin to reject that influence and to "do our own thing."

Consider some of the common sights in the countryside of the United Kingdom. "Stag-headed" oaks, for example, with their dead branches protruding through the canopy, or willows with hollow trunks from root to crown. Farther afield, ancient olives in southern Europe are similar in "style." Deadwood features such as *jins* (branches) and *sharis* (sections of trunk) are taboo on broad-leaved bonsai in Japan, but in the West they happen in real life, so why not in bonsai? However, they have to be the right kind of jins and sharis. The shapes, texture and color of traditional jins all work with conifers. The same treatment would not necessarily suit natural broad-leaved styles.

Scots pines—I've seen them from Moscow to Madrid. It's the same tree but the character changes as drastically as the climate. The now classical neo-literati style of scots pine, mastered by Peter Adams, is specific to northern Europe. I was given a pine by a Russian bonsai enthusiast who had collected it from the Caucasus Mountains in the Crimea. He had never even seen pictures of Japanese bonsai, so he had begun to train the tree in the natural low and spreading style of his area.

While on the subject of pines, what about the "umbrella" pine (*Pinus pinea*) that grows

A "Disneyesque" rendition of an old tree. The image could hardly be simpler, but what it conveys says so much about the tree—its age, character and even whether or not it's friendly!

along the Mediterranean coast? Now, there's a typically Western style just waiting to be developed, analyzed and perfected!

The aerial-rooting figs of the tropics have natural habits not found in any Japanese species nor, therefore, in Japanese bonsai. Yet many highly regarded examples are produced by fine bonsai artists. These images are deeply rooted in their psyche, but do they mean as much to us, or are they merely interesting? Since the natural growth habit that these bonsai echo is entirely alien to us, I suggest the latter is true.

Now, you may be content having an interesting bonsai, but I suspect that if you are still reading this you are more ambitious than that. If you are anything like me, something about trees touches your soul. It stems from somewhere in the subconscious—childhood memories of sights, sounds and smells. Every time you work on a tree this is reflected in your work until, eventually, it reaches out and touches the soul of others.

We should learn the techniques that help the Japanese achieve the results they get with their bonsai, and apply this knowledge to create trees that suit our own cultural tastes and reflect our own environment and our emotions toward it. We will then be free to interpret the natural shape, growth habit and, above all, spirit of our native species in bonsai form, and to do so in a way that is readily accessible to Western and Eastern audiences.

To be visually successful, images of trees must be simplified, carefully analyzed and broken down to their basic elements.

Elms

ELMS ARE among the toughest and most forgiving of all broad-leaved species employed for bonsai. They're also one of the most rewarding.

Their alternate internodes provide the opportunity to develop fine ramification with ease, without the abrupt angularity that occurs with opposite-leaved species. Their foliage reduces dramatically with regular pinching, and they produce prolific adventitious buds as a matter of course. They will tolerate extreme pruning and bounce back with all the enthusiasm of a of a child on the first day of vacation.

All elms are happy growing in containers, filling the pots with dense feeding roots within a single season, no matter how severely the old roots were cut back. Discarded sections of thick roots will often sprout new roots and shoots, providing you with even more plants to play with.

Wherever you live you will be able to find elms of some description. The information and anecdotes in this section apply to them all.

Suckers arising around the base of an ancient English elm (Ulmus procera) *in Boston Common, Boston, Massachusetts.*

In the eye of the beholder

THREE BROOM STYLES
English elm (Ulmus procera)

> **"The first attempt is always made with great care. The second builds on the lessons of the first. The third is sometimes less thoughtfully made."**
>
> Actually, this was written in 1893, by Rev. Jeremy Manleigh, in a letter that tried to dissuade a twice-widowed parishioner from marrying a younger man. But could it apply equally as well here?

UNLIKE CONIFERS, where a design can be established by reducing a dense plant and wiring the prolific shoots into position, deciduous species take longer to develop. They must be built from scratch because the branches are less supple and generally less finely ramified. Twisting and contorting branches to bring foliage masses into line may sometimes be acceptable on conifers because they're hidden from view for one thing, and are not entirely unnatural for another. But on deciduous species the integrity of the branch structure is of paramount importance. This can only be achieved by growing branches stage by stage—internode by internode—wiring only when necessary and directing branches by pruning as a preference whenever possible.

Naturally, the earlier in a tree's life you begin training, the more control you have and the less evidence of your interference will be

1981. Talk about doing things the hard way...! I had been growing this elm for seven years and it had only developed this far. Mind you, I thought it was wonderful at the time! My patience and persistence were to pay off later.

visible. But to most people in this frantic world of e-mail, home entertainment centers and frozen gourmet dinners, that's too long a haul. On the one hand, a larger plant often gives you a mature-looking trunk to start with. On the other hand, you have to disguise your work and live with the faults. On the other, other hand...you could compromise and start with something in between. So what do you do? All of the above!

Starting small: June 1974

On day one of my love affair with bonsai I scooped up a tiny elm sucker from Holland Park in London. It was mid-June and the sucker had only sprouted that spring, so the stem was still green. It had four leaves and about nine inches (22cm) of parent root—thinner than a pencil. How it survived is anybody's guess, but it did survive and is still thriving today.

In those days I knew absolutely nothing about bonsai. I had seen some small pine in Selfridge's department store (sold for indoor growing!), so I thought all bonsai were that size. Then I bought my first book. The author was pictured holding a tiny twig with a few weak roots dangling from the bottom. The caption read something like: "An oak bonsai ready for root pruning." Okay, I was convinced. I compared the picture with my one-year-old elm and thought: "Hmm, I'm not doing so badly..."

My next bonsai reading matter was a photocopy of a Brooklyn Botanic Gardens publication. There was a photograph of what appeared to be a real deciduous tree in winter. The caption said it was a bonsai that had been cared for by the same family for many generations. This was fantastic—this was *real* bonsai! The bottom of the caption had been missed by the photocopier, so I didn't read the line that gave the size and I naturally assumed that this was the same size as the cheap pines and the silly oak. "Wow! How can they make all those tiny twigs on something only nine inches (22cm) tall?" I thought about it and eventually decided that if they could do it, so could I.

For the next four or five years I built the branches internode by internode. I had worked out exactly how I wanted the branches to grow and pruned to appropriate buds from the very beginning. There were a few changes of mind along the way but, in general, it went according to plan. By 1981 it was beginning to look like a tree, or so I managed to convince myself. I had accumulated several little plants by then and I'd even built an elaborate staging and shadery for them!

I began to understand why some shoots were more vigorous than others, and how to equalize the vigor by delaying pruning on weak shoots. I had managed to reduce the original parent root to a more reasonable size and to induce strong roots from the base of the stem (it still wasn't big enough to qualify as a trunk!). The steady, almost routing development of the outer branches continued year by year until, in 1987, the tree had finally arrived. Sure, the trunk was still a little too slender, but the pro-

By 1987 the tree had finally arrived. Although I was perfectly happy with the proportions, I wasn't so keen on the pot.

portions of height, spread and height of trunk were exactly right to my eye. From this point on, I had to learn how to maintain the same size and structure while still permitting enough growth each year to sustain the tree. This is an entirely different discipline from design and development, and one that has to be adjusted to accommodate the idiosyncrasies of individual trees.

Two years later, while I was preparing the tree for an exhibition, I scraped away the old moss in order to apply some fresh. I could have kicked myself—all these years I had been looking at the wrong side of the tree! It didn't matter one iota which way round it was as far as the

"AIR WIRING"

Now, here's something you won't find in many books. Normally I'm a stickler for neat wiring but sometimes there are better, if less aesthetic, ways. Besides, it's the result that counts, and if we occasionally resort to rogue techniques, what does it matter?

It's better to position an embryonic branch when it's young than to wait until it has lignified (become woody). When the branch is fully developed, it won't have that "rainbow curve" as it leaves the trunk. Secondary and tertiary branches are also better started this way. How often have you tried to realign a secondary branch and split the fork? But when you're dealing with green and growing shoots, normal wiring is also risky. They're likely to snap off at the base, they often collapse under

pressure during the wiring process, and they often thicken so rapidly, the wire can cause scars almost overnight.

Air wiring is designed to guide a shoot in the desired direction with the minimum of contact. The branch will be shaped later by pruning, but initially you must get the first section right. You need to anchor the wire firmly, but as soon as you reach the shoot, shape the wire in a spiral, but without making contact anywhere. This is awkward at first, but with a little practice you'll soon be able to wire a perfect spiral in midair—a new party trick! By manipulating this spiral, you can aim the shoot in your chosen direction by altering the angle between it and the trunk or branch with relative safety. You can also introduce curves if you wish, but the main purpose is to establish the first few internodes.

"Air wiring"— undignified but effective.

The new front. Although I grow all my deciduous bonsai primarily for the winter image, I also enjoy them in summer. The leaves are now minute and dense, giving the tree an air of maturity and strength—even though it's only around nine inches (23cm) tall.

branches were concerned because they had been designed "in the round." But at the former back of the tree, the *nebari* (visible roots) were vastly superior to those at the old front, which had an unfortunate swelling where the remains of the original parent root were inextricably attached. I did not hesitate to reverse the tree. All I had to do was cut away one branch from the new front to expose the trunk and adjust two at the new back to close the gap there.

I was never too happy with the shallow oval pot. I had to mound up the soil so there was enough to sustain the tree, and I've never liked this practice. I tried a variety of pots but couldn't find one I liked. I did notice, however, that the trunk seemed to thicken more when deeper pots were used. Interesting....Finally, I found the right pot. It's a wonderful little pot by Bryan

In winter the horticultural and visual strength of this tiny tree are clear. Notice how much the trunk has thickened over the past few years. And all those nice plump buds....

Many elms, notably English and American elms, produce leaves in a range of sizes on the same plant, depending on the vigor and location of the shoots. Young trees and less vigorous sections of older trees can have leaves that are under half the size of those on normal growth. Vigorous shoots can bear leaves at least twice the normal size. Yet unlike any other species I can think of, all leaves are alike in color, texture and shape. This is obviously a tremendous advantage for bonsai of any size, but especially for smaller trees.

All these leaves were plucked from the same hedgerow elm within an area roughly three feet square (1m sq.).

SPUR GROWTH

Most elms bear spurlike shoots, which commonly grow from basal axillary buds on the previous year's growth or from old, weak inner twigs. Each spur bears from three to seven leaves, typically overlaid in an attractive pattern. They're also set in a horizontal plane, which you can exploit to create an elegant appearance in larger trees.

Growing trees from cuttings can give you a couple of years' head start on seedlings, but you're still able to arrange the roots precisely to form good future nebari.

Albright, with a subtle gray glaze showing tints of buff. The horizontal emphasis, enhanced by the prominent lip, makes it seem shallower than it really is and seems to give the tree a more positive base.

One step up: November 1982

By now I realized that bonsai could be bigger than nine inches, so I decided to try something a little larger. I took a couple of dozen hardwood cuttings from local hedgerows. These are easy to root in open ground over winter, and the success rate is around 80%. One cutting in particular seemed to be more ready to throw out lateral growth than the others, so I chose it for my next serious effort at a broom(ish) style. This time I decided to follow advice and let the cutting grow on in the ground for a few years to thicken the trunk and to train the main branches while in the ground.

Easier said than done! I had introduced an unfortunate kink in the trunk where I had pruned back and wired in a new leader, but I figured this would grow out or blend in with time. I also found it virtually impossible to get

1987—getting there. There's an awkward kink in the trunk where a new leader was wired in, and the inter-branch spacing is less than ideal. Fortunately, the latter problem was easily solved a couple of years later by simply removing the lower right branch.

an accurate idea of how the branches were shaping up while lying on my stomach in the mud. Nevertheless, by the time I had potted up in spring 1987, the development had almost caught up with the smaller *shohin*. Almost, but not quite. The inter-branch spacing was all awry—two close branches at the lower right and a large gap on the left toward the top. Believe it

17

1992. In summer the image is too wide, but in winter this changes. It's a subtle difference, but a significant one.

The leaves are borne in a horizontal plane. Therefore, those at the sides protrude, visually increasing the width. The leaves on the apex are also horizontal, so they have no dimensional effect.

January 2000. Now in its new pot, by David Jones of Walsall Studio, the stark winter image is most impressive. The trunk, branches and twigs have all fattened, improving the proportions.

THE SPHAGNUM WRAP TECHNIQUE

The immediate external environment around a trunk seems to have an effect on the bark. With the exception of Betula, which are colonizers of open ground and develop silver bark when grown with their trunks exposed to full sun, most trees develop mature bark more quickly when their trunks are surrounded by vegetation. The constantly moist ambience, where the bark is protected from the scarifying effects of the elements, can dramatically accelerate the process. This is especially true when trunk expansion is slow, as it is likely to be when the tree is competing with surrounding vegetation for nutrients.

We can simulate these conditions on a bonsai or on bonsai material of any age or size to improve the bark texture in the following way:

1. With a piece of coarse sandpaper very gently stroke the trunk in a vertical direction once or twice to penetrate the outermost "skin." Don't go as deep as the cambium (the green intrface between bark and wood) and remember that you're not trying to remove the skin, just to score it in a few places. Go as high on the trunk as you can and, if possible, include any heavy lower branches.

2. Take some moist sphagnum moss (or any other dead, water-retaining vegetable matter) and pack 20mm layer *loosely* around the scored area. Hold the moss in place with twine, wire or open mesh of some sort, making sure it's not compacted at all.

3. Keep the moss wet at all times, even if this means placing the tree in the shade and heaping extra moss around the trunk in dry weather. Inspect the trunk every month or so to make sure you're not inadvertently layering it! If you see roots forming, break them off and remove the moss for a few days, replacing it as soon as the bark appears dry.

This procedure prevents the normal drying and erosion of the outer "onion-skin" layers and allows moisture to soak into and expand the still-porous spent phloem. The time required for fissures to appear will depend on the thickness of the existing bark itself and the

In this close-up you can see the very convincing texture that developed on the elm after undergoing the "sphagnum wrap" technique.

Just look at the bark on this shohin hawthorn. It took three years to develop from an entirely smooth beginning. This trunk is only just over an inch (25mm) thick now. Before the bark swelled, it was half that thickness.

amount of new phloem produced during the process, but be prepared to keep the "sphagnum-wrap" in place for up to two years, possibly longer.

Allow the tree to bear as much foliage as possible to maximize the phloem production. Balancing this need with the need to maintain shape can be tricky, but even if you have to spend a year or two re-refining the branches, the improvement that mature bark will bring to your tree will be well worth the wait.

Here you can get a clearer idea of the relative sizes of the first two elms and can compare their aesthetic merit. Is the former a factor in the latter? Is the smaller tree better artistically, or is it just my imagination? Is the bigger tree superior because of its bark and the increased detail?

From the side, the apex is seen to lean forward, which creates an illusion of greater size when viewed from the front (see page 96).

or not, it actually took me three years to realize that by cutting off the lower right branch, the problem would go away!

Between 1990 and 1992 there was dramatic development, and I'm pleased to say that it was all my own work. I noticed that young trees whose trunks were constantly smothered with damp vegetation, such as coarse grasses or heathers, developed swollen, fissured bark at a

very early age. I wondered if I could simulate this on a bonsai. Looking closely at the wild trees, I could see all manner of wildlife crawling around in the crevices of the bark. There was a "healthy" smell about it all—one of a living microenvironment, not one of decay. There was also a fair amount of sphagnum moss mixed in with the other vegetation. Hmm....And so the Sphagnum Wrap technique was born. This actually works, but not overnight. It may take a few years to have any effect, but it's ten times faster than waiting for Mother Nature to do it.

This tree took only ten years to arrive, compared with thirteen for the shohin. Sure, that's only three years less, but it was twice as big and had three times as many shoots. And then there was that lovely bark, too. It still wasn't perfect, of course, but the now familiar annual maintenance and improvement program was beginning, so the slightly unruly twigs would become more orderly.

The years of disciplined pinching, pruning and planning rolled by. You get so familiar with these trees that the decision-making process becomes almost subconscious. You still have to think, but you don't have to *stop* and think. You can work faster, moving the shears from one snip to the next in one fluid movement. I'm sure the Japanese have a word for this, but I don't know what it is. All I know is that the pleasure and spiritual benefit I gain from its therapeutic value make the long years of waiting for this stage worth every second.

The big one: November 1989

I was lucky enough to attend the first World Bonsai Convention in Omiya, Japan, in April 1989. What an experience! It seemed as if every bonsai lover in the world was there—and most probably were. People whose names were bonsai household words shared their experiences and their joy with us humbler beings. One aspect of the basement exhibition room that captured my imagination was a magnificent old *hokidachi* (broom style) zelkova. On the wall beside the tree was a photograph of the tree in 1955. Forty-four years earlier! Before I was even born! Something about the concept of how these trees are slowly improved over the years by their custodians moves me.

I wanted a tree just like that zelkova, and by November that year I had one—or the beginnings of one, at least. My only regret is that I didn't take photographs of the early stages of its development. My only excuse is that it was the biggest tree I had ever had, and I couldn't move its training box single-handed. A lame excuse, but there you go....

It was a fifteen- or sixteen-year-old elm growing by the side of a local lane. The trunk was the right thickness and there was a cluster of lateral branches at about knee height. I could easily see that by cutting out the leader and shaping the wound, then doing the same to the branches at strategic points, I could make a good basic framework of short limbs on which to build. It was growing on a six-inch (15cm) thick parent root, which had to come out with the trunk, and that's hard work. Elm roots are soft and pulpy, and no tool yet invented will cut them efficiently. I generally find that brute force works better than kindness.

This elm stayed in a large growing box for four years, during which time the branches were grown on in cycles of rapid extension and hard pruning (see page 28). It was planted into a Bryan Albright pot in spring 1995 and it, too, had arrived. Only six years this time!

To be fair, it has only had five years' routine improvement. But the trunk of a tree that size should have fissured bark—which I can and will make happen. That will take about three years.

LEFT: The hokidachi *zelkova exhibited at the first WBFF convention in Omiya, Japan, in 1989.*

BELOW: A photograph of the same zelkova taken in 1955.

The nebari is also very poor because it is mostly old parent root. I could graft new roots onto the base of the trunk. That will take another five or six years to work effectively—a lot longer for the evidence of the unions to disappear completely. But will it ever be as good as either of the others? Will it ever be better?

Good and better are subjective concepts and, as such, liable to change with fashion, mood or experience.

1995. After only six years, this large, 33-inch (85cm) tall elm had reached the same stage that the others took thirteen and ten years, respectively, to reach.

21

This section of a hornbeam trunk was developed after a sequence of four growth and hard pruning cycles in successive years, as indicated by the colored pointers.

FINDING THE LINE

Reducing larger material to a manageable size almost always involves creating alternative trunk and/or branch lines. Parts of the lines are already there but the remainder must be grown, either from existing slender branch-lets or from entirely new shoots. Your problem is twofold: first, you have to decide which of the existing alternatives to use and, second, how to continue them with new growth in a fluid and convincing way.

Cutting straight across a trunk or branch any thicker than half an inch (12mm) will induce tight clusters of buds to sprout from the cambium layer, like a bright green crown. Most of these will abort within a few weeks, but some will survive. If left to their own devices, eventually one or two will become dominant and form major branches. The scar closes in time, but on a bonsai it takes a very long time!

From the side, you can see the gap where the elm's original trunk used to be, but from the front the line is entirely natural. Here again, the apex leans toward the front.

Wherever possible, it's far better to cut at an angle between two strategically placed secondary branches, preferably ones that are still slightly pliable. By controlling the shape and orientation of the scar and the direction of the secondary branches, your work will eventually become invisible. When shortening a trunk, make the sloping cut between two branches that can then be wired to make a new leader and a complementary branch. Angle the cut toward the back, so the cut surface can't be seen from the front. Make sure the line that flows along the top of the branch, up the wound and onto the new leader is fluid and echoed in the shape of the next branch and trunk section.

The elm had a cluster of four small branches growing from within a few inches of each other. Cutting out the central trunk and shortening the branches leaves a perfect basis for a broom style. Here, again, it's important to hide the wounds at the back, and to find that all-important line.

This branch was shortened and developed using the same method as for reducing the trunk on the hornbeam example. The staged cuts are now almost completely concealed beneath new tissue.

Epilogue

All three trees have more or less reached the maximum density possible in their respective containers, so I'm perfectly happy now to allow them to remain settled in their annual cycles and to embark on no further structural alterations to the branches—apart from an occasional re-build of the outer internodes. The trees are happy with this arrangement too; they seem to have found a comfortable rhythm. I've watched their patterns change over several decades as they pass through different stages: branch building, ramification, refinement. Next I want to see what twenty years of growth stasis will do for them.

Now only subtle changes take place each year, as wounds heal and the bark gradually changes in character. Whenever I spend time with them, pruning or pinching, I always see some change—subtle nuances in the character of the branches, trunk or nebari. It's a curious notion to know that others will be feeling precisely the same about these three trees long after my bones are jinned!

Summer 2000. Denser than it was five years ago, the outline is now more clearly defined.

November 2000. In winter the truth is revealed. The original branch reductions are beginning to integrate well with the newer growth, although some evidence is still visible if you look closely. The branch lines need to be cleaned, and many wayward twigs and spindly branches need to come out. I'd like to introduce some negative areas that will make the tree appear bigger. Then there's adding texture to the bark, improving the nebari, perhaps...

A gardener's legacy

BUILDING ON A HOLLOW STUMP
English elm (Ulmus procera)

You don't have to hike across mountains to find good yamadori. In fact many species don't grow in such remote places. Just keep your eyes wide open and your gaze lowered wherever you go.

To MAKE life easier for bonsai artists, English elm reproduces by throwing up hundreds of suckers from the spreading roots. These form the basis of most hedgerows and are always responsible for the patches of scrub and saplings around neglected parks and open spaces, in cities as well as in the countryside. Needless to say, for this very reason they are not popular with gardeners and park keepers, other than as a source of free beanpoles. And it is with beanpoles that this story begins....

For several years I rented an allotment—a small plot of fertile land in a community garden—where I planted out all those odds and ends that most bonsai growers accumulate. The allotment area was bordered by a mixed hedgerow of elm, ash (*Fraxinus exelsior*) and hawthorn (*Crataegus monogyna*). The hawthorns provided anti-cat barriers and the ash and elm

THOUGHT FOR THE DAY

It's that old question of age again....

If this stump is now, say, 45 years old, the parent root from which it originally sprouted as a sucker—and which now forms the nebari—may be anything up to a hundred years old. Yet the tree itself has only been growing independently on its own set of roots for a decade and a half.

So how old is the tree?

yielded the beanpoles. Each year, as the gardeners cut a fresh supply, they were doing exactly what commercial bonsai growers do to produce those thick, tapered trident maples. The only drawback was that they weren't doing it as well! Most of the stumps that were left after a beanpole raid were too tall to be of use. Lots of interesting movement and character, but all piled on top of a waist-high leg.

One cold January day in 1987, I pushed deep into the leafless thicket to harvest my beanpoles before anyone else got there. As I was looking for good stout poles, something interesting caught my eye. One very old and short stump had survived in the shade of its neighbors on the strength of one straight pole that had grown vigorously enough to push through the canopy and reach the light. The rotten hollow wounds on the stump were evidence of beanpole raids many years ago. It was getting dark and the ground was frozen solid. I resolved to collect the stump as soon as the ground had thawed.

In old hedgerows, field margins, even in neglected parts of public areas in the heart of town, it's always worth scratching around at ground level to see what delights have been buried by debris over the years.

When I finally managed to get a spade in the ground, removing the stump was still not as easy as I had hoped. The ground contained a mass of heavy, tangled roots belonging to all the neighboring trees and bushes. When the stump was eventually lifted, after many explanations to curious fellow allotmenteers, I discovered it was still dependent on the parent root, from which it had originally grown as a sucker. There was

You can see clearly how the gnarled and rotten stump is almost hidden at the base of the straight stem. In fact, at other times of the year it would have been easily hidden by weeds.

precious little fine root attached. However, being aware that English elm tolerates severe root pruning, I wasn't too worried about this. I knew that there was sufficient energy stored in the swollen section of the former parent root to sustain the plant until new roots could be formed.

Before planting the stump in its temporary container, I cut the stem right back to its point of origin. I angled the cut toward what I anticipated would be the back. This concealed the cut from the viewer and created some beginnings of taper at the top. I left intact three small weak shoots below the cut.

The center of the living stem had already begun to rot through to the hollow trunk below, indicating that it was pretty old. I cut a section of the stem about two inches (50mm) diameter to count the annual rings. Allowing five rings for the rotted core, the stem was twenty-eight

years old. I guessed the stump itself must have been around twice that age.

I knew that a ring of buds would form around the rim of the wound. This is the way with most deciduous species, but elms always oblige. Sure enough, by the end of April, a crown of tiny crowded shoots had begun to emerge from the cambium around the wound. More important, one tiny adventitious shoot had sprung from a rotted branch stub low on the left-hand side of the trunk. This was crucial to the design I had in mind.

That's right—even at this early stage I had a more or less firm idea of how I wanted the tree to develop. This is essential in all deciduous bonsai styling. The inspiration came from a picture in an old bonsai calendar I had saved. It was an immensely powerful image of a much larger hornbeam with a similar trunk character.

I had two priorities. First I had to grow on a

ABOVE: By June new shoots had grown, showing that the tree had survived its ordeal. At the very base of the stump a tiny shoot is emerging. That shoot was crucial to the design I had in mind.

Just look at the masses of buds bursting from the cambium around the wound. The hole in the center was my own handiwork.

new leader. Some of my students will be surprised to hear me say that because I'm constantly telling them off for continuing the leader right to the top of deciduous trees. "Deciduous trees," I say, "have an apex formed like a branch, with the limb approaching from below—you must forget all about leaders some way below the apex." So why grow on a new leader in this case? Well, the top of the trunk was almost square, even with the angled cut, so I had to develop some semblance of a tapered upper trunk. But I wanted a short, stubby section rather than a graceful extension that would be entirely out of character with the trunk base. The new leader would be allowed to grow vigorously before being cut hard back several times in order to achieve the result I was seeking.

The second priority was to nurture the small shoot growing at the lower left of the trunk. This was trickier. As the tree surged with

CURIOUSER AND CURIOUSER

I discovered an interesting idiosyncrasy while working on this tree. The callus on *Ulmus procera* behaves in a most curious way when deep hollows are concerned. First it rolls over the wound normally. But instead of continuing to roll toward the center of the hollow to form a seal, it flattens and spreads over the inner surface of the hollow at an alarming rate, covering the decaying wood with a new layer of living tissue. This may be the elm's natural way of coping with heart rot, to which the species is particularly prone. How the vascular bundles, or sap lines, accommodate this unusual behavior is something I've yet to work out.

In those days I used a bitumen-based wound sealant to cover cuts. Big mistake—it dries hard and stains the bark. It took hours of gentle picking away with a scalpel blade to remove the residue and several years for the telltale marks to disappear completely. In the final analysis it didn't really matter because the tree took a decade to reach maturity, so there was plenty of time. Needless to say, I never used bitumen sealants again!

Cross section of the hollow trunk

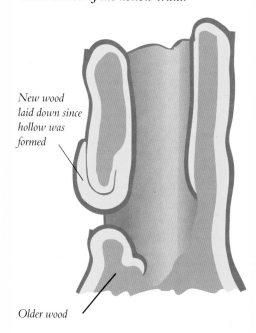

New wood laid down since hollow was formed

Older wood

In the detail of the 1987 picture you can see a large hollow with a small, tonguelike growth emerging from inside and growing upward from it. This is the end of a long ribbon of callus that has grown all the way down inside the trunk from the top of the hollow. Having found a way out, it just kept on growing, clinging to the outer surface and following its contours.

growth following the severe pruning, all the energy was going to the apex, and my precious little shoot was not doing so well. Restricting the number of shoots remaining at the apex and foliar feeding the small shoot helped it pull through. I allowed it to grow more freely and much longer than any of the other new branches, until I was confident that it could hold its own.

After five years of free growth, limited only by an annual light summer clipping to keep inner buds viable, I repotted my now vigorous and bushy elm stump into a more sympathetic container and gave it its first major pruning since collection. The low shoot had developed well and I was able at this time to treat it in the same way as all the others. By April 1992, new buds were popping out all over the short branch stubs.

However, this first pruning was not as hard

The inspiration

This photograph from an old Japanese calendar was the inspiration for my intended design. However, I always thought the new, "grown-on" leader on the hornbeam was out of harmony with the heavy trunk. I resolved not to follow this procedure with my elm, but to permit as little new leader as possible, keeping the crown low and compact.

By 1997 the hollow has reduced in diameter as calluses thicken, but the "tongue" has continued to grow, albeit more slowly than it did inside the trunk. What happens to this type of growth when the hollow is finally sealed? Take a look at the wartlike structure to the right of the hollow. All evidence of the hole through which this grew has been covered, yet the growth continues to expand slowly.

These growths also occur on mature trees, pushing their way through thick, ridged bark. Eventually, for reasons unknown, some die and shed their bark to reveal a tangled mesh of grain in the wood beneath.

Elms don't like their roots being baked in the sun or waterlogged during rainy spells, and trees in shallow pots are prone to both of these problems.

DEVELOPING BRANCHES

When growing a new set of branches on a bare trunk, one of the most crucial things to get right occurs at the very beginning of the process. While the emerging shoots are still green, select those you want to retain, and eliminate the rest. If you can't quite make up your mind, keep a few extra ones. Now use the "air-wiring" technique (wiring a loose coil around the shoot without making full contact) to aim the branch in the right direction and at the desired elevation. In a few weeks' time, this will no longer be possible.

The wire can be removed after a month or two, once the branches have set in position. Then every branch should be allowed a period of free growth, varying according to its location. Prune the upper branches very early, after they have grown three or four internodes. With luck, the first internode will be a suitable length, so you can cut back to that. If the bud faces in the wrong direction, it doesn't matter at this stage.

When wiring young shoots that you intend to develop into main branches, always shape them so that a bud is positioned exactly on the outside of each bend. This will make the forks appear more natural and will make the future restructuring easier.

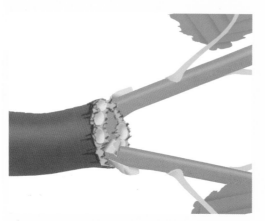

Once a branch is two or three years old, there is less need to consider the location of internodes when pruning. You can cut more or less anywhere you wish, and a new crop of adventitious shoots will be generated from the exposed ring of cambium. Two of these can be selected as arms of the first fork and they, too, will undergo the extended growth and pruning-back process until the desired thickness is achieved. To generate the strongest and most prolific crop of shoots, prune in midsummer.

It follows that, while the lower branches are developing, the upper branches become dense and highly ramified as their growth is constantly being restricted by pruning. This not only draws excessive energy from the lower branches, but it also sets them the impossible task of catching up in the future. To combat this, regularly thin out the upper parts of the tree, cutting away everything apart from a simple framework. You may even have to remove some of the very top branches entirely, at least once, and rebuild them from scratch. It won't delay the final result—it will only make it better.

Prune the second tier of branches next, when they have grown to, say, seven or eight internodes. A better indication of when to prune would be their thickness in comparison to the branches above. Prune back to the first or second internode. Continue this staggered pruning, allowing branches to become longer and thicker toward the bottom. You may well have to wait for a few years before you actually make any cuts in the lowest branches. Remember, at this stage you're only building thickness on the first section of each branch.

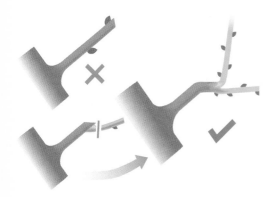

If you prune a shoot back to one bud, you'll only get one new shoot, so how do you induce the branch to fork? Well, there's a good way and a bad way. You can leave two buds when you prune and hope both will sprout. But the shoot will have no taper, and will need wiring to make a fork. It's better to cut back to one bud, then cut the next shoot off, leaving a short stub. Next year, small shoots will sprout from the dormant buds at the base of the stub and two of these can be selected to create the desired fork. The result will have greater angularity and more pronounced taper.

as it might have been. Further hard pruning followed later that year and the next. My reluctance to prune too hard at first was based on my desire to promote as many options for future branches as possible. I knew that I had pruned hard enough to induce buds on old wood, but I also wanted plenty of options on and around the newer branches and leader. Why rush decisions if doing so won't hasten the final image? Wait, consider the options, then act positively—and always have that final design firmly in mind.

At the 1992 repotting, I raised the trunk to expose the top of the old parent root. All collected *Ulmus procera* will have odd nebari. The only way to cope with them is to turn them to your advantage. In this case the nebari, such as it was, contained character and had natural hollows and features that gave the impression of great age. There were a few areas that needed to be carved out to form new hollows, but nature had done most of the work for me.

Now, I can hear you asking: "What about preserving the hollows? What if they rot right down to the roots?" To which I would reply: "What if they do?" Have you ever known heart rot in a tree to invade and penetrate the functioning sapwood until it reaches the cambium? No! It simply doesn't happen unless there is a

It is interesting to note that the bark, which was originally dark gray and rather dull, is now becoming much brighter in color. This is entirely due to its exposure to the sun and rain instead of being hidden by weeds and litter. I've also noticed that when a tree is healthy, even if it's in a small container and being constantly pinched, the bark appears much brighter and livelier. This is true of conifers as well as deciduous species. Unhealthy or weak bonsai that are not properly cared for develop this dark, lackluster bark that always looks miserable and unattractive.

parasitic fungus involved. In fact, when the stump was first collected, the hollow did run right down through the swollen parent root and emerged through a long, splitlike wound underneath. This wound has long since healed over and whatever water does accumulate inside the trunk seems to find another way out—I have no idea how.

Developing the branches

I have read many times of the danger of branches becoming too thick and heavy in proportion to the trunk, yet I confess to being unable to comprehend this suggestion. Certainly if one starts by using a thick first branch and training an opposing branch as the next section of trunk, then the first branch may well be too heavy. But it doesn't *become* too heavy, it already is. Ironically, little is written about branches being too thin—a far greater and more common problem. Branches always thicken automatically in time,

March 1992: The long years of allowing branches free growth to gain thickness were over. At last I was able to cut hard back and begin do some real construction work.

BUILDING RAMIFICATION

These photographs show the development of one small section of the lower right-hand branch of the hollow elm over three full growing seasons. You can see clearly that in my haste to achieve a full branch structure, I wired a single shoot into a series of curves in order to fill as much space as possible. I know—I advise you not to do this, yet I do it myself. No excuses. But it's only by making such mistakes that we can learn, and better you should learn from my mistakes than your own. The "snaked" section will gradually be replaced by a more credible structure.

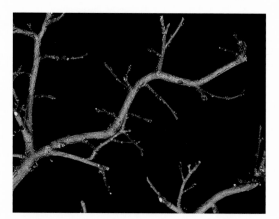

1: February 1997

4: February 1999, before pruning

5: February 1999, after pruning

but the process is very slow indeed. And, since the trunk also thickens at the same time, and often faster, the problem generally remains unresolved.

The best approach is to build the branches— step by step, internode by internode—ensuring that the length and thickness of each section is appropriately proportioned. This process certainly takes time, but it's much quicker than waiting for branches to thicken at their own lethargic pace; it creates better taper and a more angular, aged-looking structure—which is precisely what we want.

Building ramification

The constant redevelopment of the outer portions of the branches continues throughout the tree's life. This is necessary because the annual crop of shoots will gradually extend the branches. Merely cutting each shoot back to its base is not enough. This will cause large, unsightly "knuckles" to develop at the branch tips. At each pruning session, you must cut out some older parts of the outer zone, leaving space for younger shoots from neighboring twigs to develop as replacements.

At first, only small sections toward the tips will need to be cut away. Later, as the twigs become denser and branch tips thicken, you'll need to remove much larger areas. Each time you prune, you make improvements for the future.

There may be a few weeks when certain areas appear a little thin, or a season or two when more drastic reconstruction is taking place and your tree is less than perfect. But each time the tree regains its form, it is better than the last time.

By summer 1996, the shape was almost complete. The only bit of major construction that wasn't quite complete was the apex. Here I wasn't satisfied with the degree of taper, so a shoot from the back of the apex was allowed to

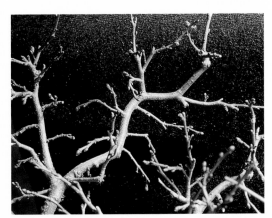

2: February 1998, before pruning

3: March 1998, after pruning

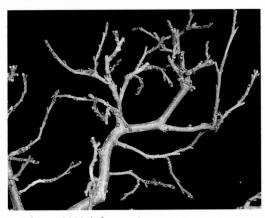

6: February 2000, before pruning

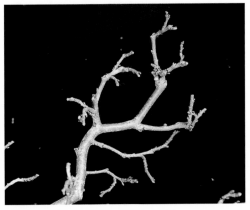

7: February 2000, after pruning

If you cut back a thick branch in the dormant season, you will get a fair number of buds around the wound and many more on even older wood. Cutting back in midsummer results in fewer buds on older wood but many more than you will ever need around the wound.

August 1996. The branches were building nicely, but the short new leader still needed to thicken. I left a long sacrifice shoot growing at the back of the new leader for two years to achieve this.

In February 1997 I was satisfied that the sacrifice shoot had done its job, so I cut it off. For the first time I could see the plan coming together.

grow freely for the whole season before being pruned away completely.

In February 1997 I cut off the sacrifice shoot, since it had by then completed its task. The branches and overall bulk were about right but more ramification was needed.

The photograph on the left was taken before the tree received its winter prune. Even at this stage of development the process of extension and selective pruning continues, albeit on a smaller scale. Each of the hundreds of shoots is pruned to a carefully chosen bud or node. Be sure to consider the next few years' growth and development before making the cut.

Several seasons of constant pinching and careful dormant pruning finally produced an established bonsai, whose true beauty can only be fully appreciated in winter, when the character of the trunk and tracery of the branches are exposed. The bark, warts, old hollows and fine, dense twigs create the impression of a really ancient tree.

The strategy

Between 1992 and 1996 I wired the main branches, guiding them into position rather than trying to introduce permanent shapes. I developed the secondary branches largely by growing on and pruning back to carefully selected buds in regular cycles, wiring them only when absolutely necessary. It's much better to use this combination of limited wiring with hard pruning whenever possible in building deciduous branches. Occasional wired curves combined with sharper, pruned angles create a far more natural and pleasing branch line. Branch lines are so important when your tree is leafless for half the year.

This principle is all the more important when you're dealing with a rugged trunk, especially when it is hollow. Nothing looks more incongruous on an ancient, battle-scarred trunk than gracefully curved branches and a delicate little *moyogi* (informal upright) perched on top to provide the apex. The tree in the picture that inspired this design displayed this flaw. The overall proportions, ramification and branch layout were beyond criticism, but the upper portion of the trunk belonged to a different tree.

I believe a strong correlation exists between what is, for want of a better word, "correct" horticulturally and narratively (in terms of the

February 2000. The twigs have now reached maximum density. Having enjoyed the winter image, it's now time to prune in readiness for the coming spring. I've already pruned the lower left-hand branch.

Four and a half hours later the pruning is finished. It takes so long to prune properly because every single cut must be carefully considered. You can't just clip the tree to shape like a hedge. That would be too easy!

Summer 2000. When the tree is in leaf, the trunk is almost hidden beneath the dense foliage. For summer display, the foliage needs to be thinned, but that would spoil it for the winter.

Ten years after being decapitated, the wounds have begun to heal and blend in with the surrounding bark.

tree's implied history) and what also appears to be "correct" aesthetically.

Hollow trunks tell us the tree reached maturity many years ago and has already begun to deteriorate. But the trunk can only tell half the story; the character of the branches tells the rest. A hollow trunk with few branches and sparse foliage tells us that this process of slow death is continuing. However beautiful, this image will always be sad. But when such a trunk is cloaked in lush foliage supported by dense twigs, the image is more exciting. It's an image of persistence, tenacity, determination. The tree has clearly been subjected to the very worst that nature can throw at it, yet it soldiers on, strong and defiant. This image excites and stimulates.

Once you have established a good framework of branches of appropriate thicknesses—and only then—you can begin the refinement of the outer zones by building up that wonderful, dense tracery of twigs that make old deciduous trees such a joy.

This is done in more or less the same way as the branch framework was built, but on a finer scale and without the staggered timing. Trim to shape in summer and prune each shoot individually and with careful consideration during the dormant season. To give you some idea of the care and attention needed during dormant pruning, when I pruned this elm in February 2000, it took me four and a half hours.

The design

Although the design generally conforms to traditional bonsai principles—a near-triangular silhouette, a heavy trunk, an alternating branch placement, etc.—it doesn't fall easily into any particular style. The trunk lacks the curves of a *moyogi* (informal upright), which is why I avoided building a silly little moyogi apex like the one pictured in the calendar. Neither is it a *hokidachi* (broom) nor a *chokkan* (formal upright). Does it matter? No.

The elms of Olde England

ELM SAIKEI

English elm (Ulmus procera)

The concept of beauty is fickle where the superficialities of human life are concerned. But with nature, in all its forms, our concept of beauty is inherited from our distant ancestors to whom nature was god.

IN THE thirteenth century, the English government passed a series of statutes compelling everyone who owned or had title to land to mark its boundaries with an enclosure—a dry stone wall or hedgerow. Traditionally, dry stone walls were used wherever suitable hedgerow trees were scarce or grew poorly, or when the boundary was intended to enclose sheep, which will eat their way through almost anything! But in lowland, sheep-free areas, hedgerows were the preferred means of enclosure. Landowners were opportunists and would use whatever species were already *in situ:* hawthorn, hazel, ash, beech, or oak. But by far the most common and effective species was the English or Field elm (*Ulmus procera,* syn. *Ulmus campestris*).

Ever since then, the landscape of southern England had been a cozy place, full of small fields, winding lanes and quiet corners that inspired many artists and poets with its charm. England's most famous landscape painter, John Constable, was a lover of elms, and his paintings are a permanent record of the English landscape as it had been for over five centuries. In his painting *The Cornfield,* one of the elms that towers above the farm boy drinking from a clear stream has a small patch of yellowing foliage. This is neither a mistake, nor poor-quality paint that has faded over time. This is evidence of Dutch elm disease, which has broken out in minor epidemics in the United Kingdom several times in the past. But nature is balanced, and because in those days man respected and worked with nature, the disease had little long-term impact.

After the Second World War, many thou-

British painter Andrew Horsewell captured the essence of the English countryside before the elms disappeared. Scenes like this are dear in the hearts of all English folk over 40 years old.

sands of miles of hedgerow had been uprooted in the lust for more efficient farming. Large mature trees had been felled by landowners, fearful of the litigation that might follow if a branch fell (which they frequently do) and caused damage to neighboring property or, worse still, a passerby.

Then, in the very early 1970s, disaster struck in the form of an outbreak of Dutch elm disease. This strain of the disease proved to be far more virulent than any that England had previously experienced and, within five or six years, scarcely a mature elm was left standing. By 1980, the death of over 25 million elm trees had been recorded. Many times that number became victims whose sudden death remained unrecorded. Acting in panic, landowners ripped up thousands of miles of perfectly healthy hedgerows, prompted by the erroneous but widely held opinion that the disease would spread through the roots. Thankfully, people now know better.

Without the majestic, billowing elms, dark and ominous against the summer sky, hosts to the inevitable colony of soaring rooks—noisy, crowlike birds that constantly squabble over their nesting sites—or the thick, spreading hedgerows, teeming with life and filling every country walk with twists, turns and surprises, the landscape of much of southern England is now bland, and uninspiring. Through self-seeking avarice and mind-blowing irresponsibility, my children and the generations to follow have been robbed of something very precious.

The destruction of the English elm, following as it did hot on the heels of my introduction to bonsai, left me with feelings of both anger and despair. I suppose it was inevitable that I should one day try to use my newly acquired skills to recreate an image and, hopefully, some of the spirit of my lost heritage.

The primary tree

The history of this *saikei*—for it is a landscape, not a group or forest planting—is a comparatively long one, starting back in 1980. At that time I was an Art Deco enthusiast and knew rather more about that than bonsai. I particularly liked the stylized images of trees used to decorate tableware of that period—tall, slender, open-crowned. Ironically, these images owed much to the influence of Japanese aesthetics.

Outside the window of the London apartment I lived in during the 1970s, stood a Wheatley elm (U. carpinifolia wheatleyi.) In 1976 I watched as first one small patch of foliage turned yellow, then brown. Within six weeks the tree was dead. Fortunately U. carpinifolia varieties do produce viable seeds and I was lucky enough to find a couple of seedlings that had germinated in the leaf litter in the basement surround. I still have one of these today—a treasured reminder.

ARMAGEDDON OF THE ELM

In 1970, motivated by commercial greed, an unscrupulous Canadian timber exporter and an irresponsible English importer conspired to flout the law. They shipped to the UK a consignment of recently felled elm trunks with the bark still attached. This one unforgivable sin was to destroy my beloved landscape forever, for concealed beneath the bark were larvae of the beetle *Scolytus scolytus*, which spreads the spores of the deadly fungus *Ceratocystis ulmi*—Dutch elm disease—as it flies from tree to tree to lay its eggs.

The disease is not limited to Dutch elms (*U.* x *Hollandica*), neither are the Dutch responsible for it. It's so called because it was first diagnosed in Holland in the 18th century.

The tiny Scolytus beetle is only one-sixth of an inch (4mm) long, yet it can cause such devastation. It has short, sturdy legs, brown wing cases and a black head and thorax. You may spot them feeding or burrowing around the collar where young branches emerge on mature trees. They tunnel galleries beneath the bark in which they reproduce twice a year, in early and late summer. The larvae tunnel outward at right angles to these galleries, feeding on the phloem. The deadly fungus thrives on the droppings of the larvae and rapidly spreads beneath the bark, eventually colonizing the entire tree and killing the cambium as it progresses. Death is very quick, usually within one season.

The beetle normally flies at around 18 – 20 ft (3 – 3.5 meters), so small saplings and bushes are not in danger. Neither are your bonsai—they are more likely to be killed by a neighbor's cat. However, in recent years, young elm of only 15 ft (5 meters) or so have become infected, so there are indications that the beetle is adapting to the change in height of its host.

Oh, dear! And to think that I was so proud of this silly elm! It's hard to imagine that this was to become the major tree in a future landscape. Novices take note: Any tree can be salvaged with a little imagination.

Oh, well, it seemed like a good idea at the time. The suckers that I'd twined around the trunk were supposed to self-graft—but no chance....

So, bravely going where no man had gone before, I lovingly trained a most unlikely-looking elm for the next few years. By 1983 I was, believe it or not, immensely proud of the result—it was just like the images I was trying to copy. Then I discovered Peter Adams's book *The Art of Bonsai*, the first book to deal with bonsai as an artistic discipline. More important, it was the first book to credit bonsai with its own aesthetic. I started looking harder at bonsai design principles and the differences between bonsai images and images of trees in other media—especially dinner plates!

I cringe when I see the photograph of that attempt now, but I'm not ashamed of it. As I tell students who are shy about showing me their work: everyone was a beginner once and beginners make all kind of mistakes. The secret is to acknowledge that you can be wrong and not be afraid to admit it by changing your mind occasionally, no matter how experienced you might become.

I did change my mind, of course, and this imitation of a 1920s table lamp was to become the major tree in the new composition, but not until I had managed to make another terrible mistake with it.

By 1984 the branches were shaped more sensibly. I had bent them down, spreading the crown, and I was encouraging dense clumps of fine shoots to grow from burls on the trunk—as real elms used to do. I also realized that to develop the tree quickly I needed to plant it in a larger container. Several suckers had emerged from just below soil level around the base of the trunk. I thought it would be a good idea to weave them around the trunk in anticipation that they would eventually graft themselves to the trunk, so to speak, and create an aged, gnarled appearance. Dumb!

After transplanting the tree into open ground and allowing it to grow vigorously for a few years, these suckers had badly marked the bark on the trunk. They showed no intention of becoming grafted on, despite the fact that the trunk had thickened considerably and the suckers were pinned to it with a staple gun. At just a few parts near the base, the suckers appeared to have grafted, but I wasn't sure of it. I was sure, however, that if I tried to remove them the resulting scars would be impossible to disguise.

I cut off the loose sections of the suckers and left the rest. This damage to the trunk made the

ELM SUCKERS

Ulmus procera virtually never produces viable seeds. It reproduces almost entirely from suckers emerging from the spreading roots. These suckers grow in clusters, generally from the undersides of roots that are close to the surface. They curl upward around the root before they emerge into the light. Only one sucker from a cluster will survive under normal circumstances. The base of the new stem fuses with the parent root, causing a swelling. Feeder roots then grow from this swelling until, eventually, the new tree develops its own entire root system. The section of root between the new trunk and the parent tree—the placenta, so to speak—may continue to serve two masters for many years. In some elm hedgerows long stretches of individual plants with trunks as thick as your thigh are all connected by (and largely dependent on) one common root.

Most elms will reproduce through suckers to some extent, as do many other species used for bonsai. Occasionally the bizarre formations at the base of the trunk have interesting characteristics that can be retained and used in the design (see the chapter "A Gardener's Legacy"). But normally this isn't the case. One's initial thoughts, based on a forgivable impatience to see an established bonsai, are often to live with the poor nebari and concentrate on the rest of the tree. I promise you, in years to come you will begin to regret this. Nothing is more frustrating than spending a decade or more perfecting the branches and ramification, only to have an ugly nebari ruin the entire creation.

I strongly recommend that your first action should always be to air-layer or thread-graft a new set of roots. Yes, this takes time—and yes, it takes even longer for the new roots to blend with the trunk. But you will be so pleased that you did it.

tree useless as a subject for a single bonsai, but being sentimental and ever hopeful, I put it back on the training bench.

The secondary tree

In 1984 I began training another elm, this time a twin-trunk plant in the "mother-and-child" style. I still believed that it was possible to train branches efficiently by using ties, weights and so on. I now believe otherwise. Such devices lack sufficient control and are much slower to take effect than conventional wiring.

By 1987 this tree was beginning to look better. Branches nicely placed, ramification going well, but what about the trunks? Trunks as thin

The secondary tree in the composition. Although it's slightly more treelike than my first attempt with the primary tree, the trunk is still far too slender. My impatience to see a "finished" result was my worst enemy in those days.

Dutch elm disease poses a danger to all species of elm, but some are less attractive to the beetle as a food source, so are misleadingly said to have a degree of immunity. Fortunately, Chinese elm (*Ulmus parvifolia*) and Siberian elm (*Ulmus pumilla*), both common bonsai subjects, are two such species.

as this are too visually weak to sustain a heavy foliage mass—it would look better in a group, I thought. A year later, the crown was looking even better, and the shallow pot suited the slender trunk. But horticulturally, maintaining a full crown in such a shallow pot proved to be a nightmare. So back it went into a larger container for a few years to try to thicken the trunk.

The hedgerow

As I said earlier, it was inevitable that I should, one day, think of creating a *saikei* in the image of my lost landscape, and it finally happened in 1989, soon after I had acquired some four-foot-long (1.25 meter) oval fiberglass trays. But first I needed suitable material for the hedgerow.

Wherever there is English elm, there is a profusion of young suckers. Sometimes you can actually trace the course of the root system by following the clear lines of suckers. It didn't take much searching around the edge of my allotment to find a four-foot-long section of root bearing eighteen clusters of suckers. I replanted the root in a series of hairpin bends in a jumbo-sized seed tray until it developed a good new root system and sturdier trunks. Work on the shaping of the individual elements

of the hedgerow began almost immediately.

Traditionally, hedgerows were periodically "layed." This involved partially cutting through all the vertical trunks at about chest height. They were then bent down at the cut and woven through the adjacent trunks to form a dense living fence. I soon discovered that this was not at all easy on a minute scale. Each time I tried, most of the woven shoots died back and were replaced by new ones growing from below. However, a sufficient number survived the operation to form a good basis for further development.

The assembly

I assembled all the elements of the *saikei* in 1992, adding a third, more distant tree I had grown from a cutting. I planted this beyond the brow of the hill to suggest that the pattern of hedgerows with their occasional mature trees was continued. I think it's important in bonsai landscape design not to create "hard edges" to the composition. A bonsai landscape is a section, a sample, of a much greater whole and the space around it (and through it) should imply that, rather than act as a frame does to a painting. The viewer should feel a part of that greater

After assembling the landscape, I crammed it into the training area with all the other junk. I allowed all the elements free rein for a season so the roots could get established. Even so, by August all the plants showed signs of stress due to the excessively coarse, inorganic soil I had used. Elms prefer a soil with at least 40% organic matter.

whole. In this sense, the space can be as important as the plants and other elements, if not more so.

I intentionally broke one of the golden rules of bonsai planting by mounding up the soil. This wasn't done for the usual reason, to accommodate a deep root system, but to create the illusion of distance. Planting the third, smaller tree beyond the hill completed that illusion.

A hill like this uses a lot of soil which, in turn, can hold an awful lot of water. During the first year it became evident that my standard peat and grit mix allowed the outer two or three inches (5–8mm) to become dry enough to damage the feeding roots. Meanwhile, the central core remained very wet—in spite of the more than adequate drainage holes I had made in the fiberglass tray. This problem became worse as the masses of very fine roots that this species naturally produces in pot culture began to fill the pores and air spaces. That was a difficult year, with much digging around to check on moisture content on an almost daily basis and watering slowly and carefully.

The following spring I changed all the soil, replacing the original with a mix of 20% calcined clay (baked clay granules) and pumice with 80% grit to form a free-draining, root-friendly mound. That soil proved to be ideal and is still in use today.

Repotting is a big job, requiring four hands and several hours, but thanks to the large volume of soil it's only necessary every three years. All my other elms are repotted annually because of the high density of fine roots they produce. It's essential with most elms to eliminate a high proportion of these very fine roots that form like coconut fiber matting in the pot. If you allow these to build up year after year, they will eventually become so dense that water can't penetrate, and this has serious consequences.

By 1994 the plants were developing rapidly. The major trees were taking full advantage of the vastly increased soil mass in which their roots could grow. Trunks had thickened and branch ramification was greatly improved. The only problem was that the free-draining soil was also free-moving. Each time I watered, no matter how gentle I tried to be, the surface particles

The centerpiece of my display at the British convention in 1997. At first I was wary of showing a bonsai without a visible container, but none of the inevitable passing pedants made adverse comments. I guess that means the idea worked!

Elms don't like their roots being baked in the sun or being waterlogged during rainy spells, and trees in shallow pots are prone to both of these problems.

In spite of the size of the composition and the fact that its display had no arbitrary boundary imposed upon it by a container, the eye is always drawn through the gateway, along the cart track and over the brow of the hill. This scene touches something deep in the soul, some primeval urge to explore, to wander, to seek new pastures.

table and mounding dull gray grit right over the rim enabled me to extend the moss, breaking the outline of the tray and, in effect, increasing that all-important, visually powerful space around the image, further implying that it was part of a greater whole.

Normally when applying moss to bonsai soil one would arrange small areas of different species. Here I wanted large areas of "pasture." Luckily, I have a secret location where I can collect slabs of healthy moss up to two feet (600mm) across. It lies beneath some high-tension electricity pylons where the ground is covered with coarse, compacted fuel ash to suppress weed growth and allow easy access for the engineers. Every couple of years the area is sprayed with Paraquat, a weed-killer that destroys all vegetation on contact with the leaves—except moss. (Japanese gardeners note!)

Having seen the *saikei* displayed in this fashion now causes me to question whether, in a display, an orthodox container is always essential. Of course any bonsai must be grown in a container, but the image created by hiding the container in this way adds a new dimension that has its own distinct virtues.

in areas not covered by moss were disturbed. No moss could form naturally on these areas and the moss surrounding them was quickly washed away. On the training bench, I experimented with transplanting thick slabs of moss together with up to an inch (25mm) or more of backing soil. This seemed to work.

The *saikei* is still in the fiberglass tray, although I'm far from happy with it. I favor a large slab extending a little all around the edges of the soil. Finding a natural stone slab this size—and of manageable weight—is virtually impossible, so the next stage will be to construct one with reinforced high-alumina cement *(see page 46)*.

By 1997 the trees and hedgerow were refined enough to exhibit, but the container was not up to standard. The opportunity arose for me to mount a display at the National Bonsai Convention in Bournemouth, UK. I wanted to make this display different and decided to use this saikei as the centerpiece. But somehow I had to overcome the problem of the undignified container.

Raising the tray three inches (75mm) off the

Aesthetic considerations

There is a theory among artists that one of the elements that make for a successful landscape painting is the inclusion of hints of habitation such as the edge of a cottage peeping out from behind the trees, partially obscured gateways and lanes or a stream disappearing under a bridge. Features like these offer an imaginary place of refuge from which the landscape can be surveyed while the viewer is out of sight of enemies or predators. They invite the viewer to travel into the picture—to see around the corner, involving the viewer in a very personal interaction with the picture.

In spite of the considerable bulk of the two major trees in this composition, and the interest created by the landscaping of the hedgerow and moss, the viewer is drawn along the cart track, through the gateway and is ultimately left wondering what lies beyond the brow of the hill. At either side of the composition, rather than merely coming to an abrupt end, the hedgerow curves away from the viewer and disappears over the lower slopes of the same hill, implying there is more to see.

English elm—saikei

January 2000

**30 inches (75cm) high; 48 inches (120cm) wide.
Temporary container**

What you see—trees, hedgerow, hill, cart track—creates the setting. What you don't see creates the magic.

Close to the edge

FOREST ON A HILLSIDE

Zelkova serrata

Bonsai design is usually reactive—you respond to the tree in front of you. But sometimes it can be proactive, when you seek out plants to suit a preconceived plan.

WHEN I WAS a comely youth, I spent many a Sunday cycling through the hills and dales of southern England. One of my favorite routes took me through the chalk downs of Berkshire and Buckinghamshire—rolling hills covered in a patchwork of fields, hedgerows and woods. The wooded areas were confined most-ly to the steeper slopes and consisted almost entirely of beech (*Fagus sylvatica*). Beech are one of the few trees that thrive in chalky soils, and here they grew immensely tall, with straight slender trunks and high, arching branches. Cycling or walking beneath them was like pass-ing through a gigantic cathedral whose columns and vaults dwarfed mere humans.

I was also fascinated by the seasonal changes that took place. Not so much in the trees them-selves because, from below, you don't see much of them. It was the total change in the ambience below the trees that captivated me. In summer it was cool and dark, with hardly a single break in the canopy to let in the sunlight. Only a few understorey plants could exist in such deep shade but, nevertheless, the ground was covered in lush green. One could hide and never be found. In fall, as the copper-hued leaves fell and carpeted the earth, the canopy became progres-sively less dense and the low sun made the ground glow with vibrant color. In winter, espe-cially when there was snow, the woods were open and drafty. The gray trunks were almost the same color as the heavy sky that seemed to come down to meet them. And then spring warmth would wake them from their rest. The light became filtered and tinted gold by the newly emerging leaves, and a magical carpet of bluebells appeared almost overnight. Paradise!

So it should come as no surprise to learn that I had always wanted to re-create something of that ambience in bonsai form. Beech were out of the question. Their leaves are always rather large and the growth is coarse—long internodes and fairly thick shoots. I could have used my favorite broad-leaved species, English elm, but I have plenty of those already. Besides, my experience tells me that their incredibly dense roots are difficult enough to deal with on a single tree. A forest on a hillside would be inviting problems. In the end, I settled on zelkova because of the bark color and the very fine, straight shoots that develop after a few years' refining. These shoots are easier to con-trol and organize in a forest context than the more wayward elm shoots.

It took two years to find enough young zelkovas with straight trunks and of varying thicknesses. Even now, I would prefer to have had some a little thicker, but the glory of forest plantings is that you can always substitute plants every now and again—nothing is static.

I had the trees growing merrily away in flowerpots, but what could I do about the hill-side? I had considered using a flat Devon rustic slate that I had lying around. It had beautiful tints of blue and rust as well as an interesting texture. But it was as flat as a pancake. I wanted something with a little more character, more natural perspective—more "landscapey." I had played around at making cement slabs in the past and I was pretty confident that I could manufacture something suitable, so I decided on that course.

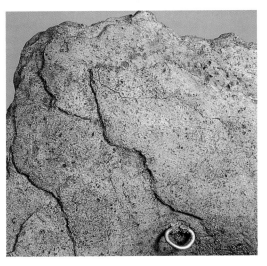

My purpose-built concrete slab. The surface has weathered beautifully and the texture and color are excellent. The wire loop, which will help anchor the trees, is glued into a shallow hole.

Once I had made up my mind to construct a cement hillside, a whole new world of possibilities opened up for me. I could dictate size, shape, texture, angle—everything. Such creative freedom is all very well, but it needs to be tamed by some rationale. The first consideration was, in fact, the weight because I have little interest in producing anything I can't lift on my own. This, in turn, limited the size. Now I had a starting point.

The next consideration was the angle. Not only the inclination of the hillside, but also the angle at which it would be presented to the viewer. A flat, straight-on sloping slab wouldn't work for me. I wanted to look through the forest from one end to the other, as one would when walking through it, not gaze at it from the opposite side of the valley. This meant that the slab had to be viewed almost end-on.

Next, the shape. Viewing the slab from one end would limit the view of the distant trees, and I wanted to be able to see them, so that their size—therefore their distance—would register. Answer? A curved slab that could be viewed from one end but would become more face-on at the far end.

Making the slab thinner at the distant end enhanced the perspective. I also made it slightly more horizontal at that end, to imply the floor of the valley. The farther away the hillside was, the more of the surrounding terrain would be in the field of vision, so this seemed logical.

IN NEED OF SUPPORT

At first I was concerned that the need to support the curved slab in an elevated position somehow made the composition false or contrived. Surely, if it wasn't a self-supporting structure, it was breaking the rules.

Then I thought about cascades, which also need special supports. They can't just be stood on the bench, because the lowest point falls below the base of the pot. So if a cascade bonsai needs special treatment, why not my forest on a sloping slab?

At present, the slab is supported by a piece of concrete, but in the future I'll make a more dignified structure.

CONCRETE CONTAINERS

What kind of cement?

Ordinary portland cement is perfectly strong enough for this work if properly reinforced. However, it takes several days, possibly weeks, to become dry enough to handle without crumbling or risking hairline fractures.

It's far better to use a quick-drying cement. There is a product marketed under various brand names in many countries called "Ciment Fondue." It has a variety of uses ranging from rapid repair work to sculpture, but it's not always readily available. All Ciment Fondue consists of is, basically, what builders and engineers call high alumina cement (or high aluminum cement, depending on where you live). This is much easier to obtain from any decent builders' supply store. It hardens sufficiently for the workpiece to be handled in twenty minutes to an hour.

All cement products take many weeks to cure—for all significant traces of moisture to disappear and to achieve maximum strength. Quick-drying cement hardens more quickly, thus allowing the work to be used, but it doesn't cure any more quickly. So, although the container can be handled confidently within a day, it shouldn't be used for planting for at least three months.

Reinforcement

Reinforced concrete derives its strength from the combined high-compression strength of both the concrete and the high-tensile strength of the steel reinforcement. In terms relevant to this discussion, imagine a slab of concrete of any thickness with a steel wire running through its center. If force is applied to its surface, for the slab to break, the wire must be stretched and the concrete above it must be compressed. This can't be done, so the slab is strong (*diagram A*).

Now, if the wire is almost at the surface when the pressure is applied, for the slab to break, the wire must be compressed or merely bent and the concrete stretched. The slab is easily broken (*diagram B*). Ideally you need a galvanized steel mesh with, say, a one-inch (25 mm) grid. Then find some synthetic fiber netting, like tulle, for example.

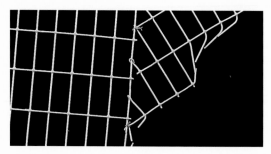

Cut the mesh to size and mold it to the desired shape. Keep your first attempt simple. Join two or more pieces together or cut out wedge sections in order to bend a single piece to the desired shape. Avoid any overlaps and remove all excess wire and loose ends. Too many wires bunched together will create a weak point. Free ends around the rim should be bent to form a more or less continual line, allowing for about three eighths of an inch (9mm) of cement to be applied before the final dimension is reached.

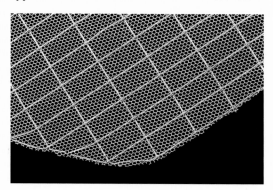

Coat the wire with quick-drying spray adhesive and smooth the netting over the mesh, ensuring it sticks reasonably uniformly, especially around the edges. It doesn't need to form a really firm bond, just enough to stay put for the time being. Don't let the netting overlap where sections are joined; better, leave a small gap. Trim the edges flush with the mesh and wait till dry.

TIP! Add the water to the cement little by little until you get the hang of it. When the mix is almost wet enough, only add a tiny amount more water. At this consistency, one or two drops more water can make an enormous difference.

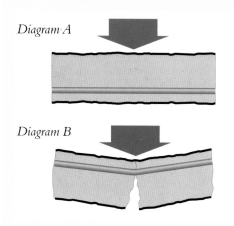

Diagram A

Diagram B

Now mix the cement

Check to see if the product is already mixed with sand or not. If not, mix well with an equal amount of dry builder's sand, the type used for mortar. Add water, stirring continually, until the mix is what I can only describe as a cake-mix consistency. Too much water will weaken the mix; too little makes it impossible to work properly in this context. If it is thin enough to brush on, it's too thin—start again.

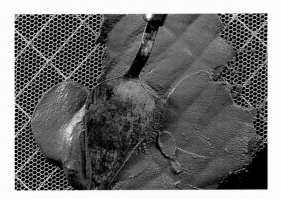

Using a trowel or palette knife, spread a layer of cement over the netting. Press firmly enough to force it through the holes in the netting.

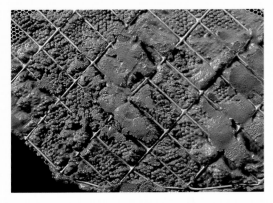

As the cement passes through the netting, it spreads a little. Once it begins to harden, it holds fast. The same effect happens around the wire as well. Every so often, reach underneath and gently spread any cement that has penetrated the netting so far that it makes mini-stalactites.

As cement is applied, it adds weight and the mesh will begin to bend out of shape. To minimize this, support the work from below with wedges. First, work around the edges, and stop as soon as the mesh begins to distort. Wait until the first section has become firm and then fill in the remaining areas, bit by bit.

Before each section hardens, gently wipe the surface with a dry, rough cloth to provide a fine key for the subsequent layer.

When the first application begins to lighten in color, very carefully lift the piece and turn it over, supporting it as necessary. Immediately begin to apply cement to the second side, ensuring that it is worked into the spaces created by the pattern of netting and mesh. It is important that these two layers meet and bond perfectly. If you have to do this layer in sections, make the joints in different places from those in the first layer, thus avoiding any weak spots.

As you work around the edges, begin to extend the rim beyond the mesh framework. When the slab is finished, the cement should extend beyond the wire by about three eighths of an inch (9mm).

The next layer is applied to the first side, so you'll have to turn the piece over again. Remember that although it's getting heavier, it isn't yet very strong. The semi-dry cement will crack if handled thoughtlessly.

This layer can vary in thickness to create a stonelike surface, say from one-eighth to one-quarter inch (3 – 6mm). If the base layer has become dry, spray it thoroughly a few times with water before you begin. The final layer on each side is the one where you will create the surface texture. You can sculpt it with the palette knife; you can add sand or grit (never more than 25% or the surface may weaken); you can press peat or turf roots into the surface or stipple it with a wire brush—whatever suits your fancy.

You can incorporate cement dyes if you wish. but don't overdo it. The idea is to make the slab look natural. Too much texture or too strong a color will make that already difficult task impossible.

When this final layer has become firm on both sides, you can color the surface with very diluted spirit-based paint or wood stain, applied in several thin coats. This will soak into the surface of the uncured cement and will be virtually permanent.

Leave the slab outdoors so the rain will wash the surface clean of colorant residues. Some sources recommend sealing the cement to stop lime from entering the soil. These days, there is little significant free lime in cured concrete. Anyhow, if you make your slab in the autumn and leave it out in the weather all winter, it will be ready for planting come spring.

The cement mix is spread onto the frame in layers, each of which must be applied before the previous layer has cured, ideally before it has even begun to change color from dark (wet) to light (dry) gray. If you have to leave the job standing overnight between layers, cover it with wet cloth and then a sheet of plastic to prevent the surface of the cement from losing moisture to the atmosphere.

RIGHT: I wired some stripped alder twigs onto the wire loops to make a rigid framework on which to lash the trees.

BELOW: Tying the trees in place was a tricky affair, made all the more so by the fact that the soil kept sliding down the slab.

A forest is born

Before I could plant up my forest, I had to devise a way of preventing the trees from sliding down the hill the first time it rained. I drilled shallow holes in the central area of the slab and glued wire loops in them with epoxy resin. Then I stripped the bark off some alder twigs. I chose alder because it is fairly slow to rot under the soil. I then made a kind of snowshoelike framework by wiring these twigs to the loops.

My thinking behind this was that I could initially tie the trees to the twigs with raffia. The raffia would decay within a season, so it would not risk cutting into the roots or lower trunks. By the time the raffia had rotted, the roots would have enmeshed with the twigs, so they would be self-supporting. When the twigs themselves had finally decayed, the roots would have become sufficiently dense for the loops alone to hold the trees firm. So far, so good....

While I was waiting for the slab to weather, I experimented with maintaining a small group of zelkova on the sloping Devon rustic slate, just to see what the practical problems might be. The only real difficulty was finding a way to water the planting without washing away the soil. In the end, I found that if I watered it from behind, so that the only water that fell directly onto the soil was dripping from the leaves, the problem was solved. Most of the water entered the soil along the top edge and soaked down through the hillside to drain away at the foot. Just like in real life!

I assembled the forest slowly, taking three evenings to complete the job. I had never tackled anything quite like this before and I'd seen nothing else like it, so I had no point of reference apart from the image in my mind. By the time the job was finished, I was reasonably satisfied. Of course there were a few annoying faults—there always are, but nothing too serious.

For one thing, the edges of the landscaping are a little too uniform—more undulation is needed, in spite of the fact that there is already a gully separating the middle ground from the distant. Also, when viewed from certain angles,

LEFT: The planting is almost complete.

RIGHT: Once the edges of the soil had been secured with clay and peat slurry, I completed the landscaping with coarse akadama. This is delightfully open and ideal for the surface— especially considering how quickly water will have to penetrate before it runs off.

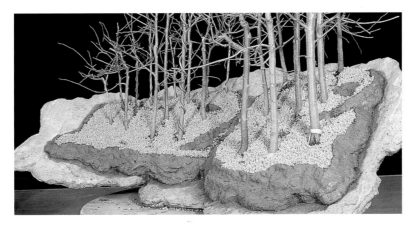

ABOVE: I saved the traditional clay-and-peat wall until last. I find it easier to plaster the edges of the soil with this mixture after planting, than to build a dinky little wall at the outset. The slurry mingles with the outer soil particles and forms a more cohesive perimeter in the long term.

The completed planting. The soil is covered with fresh moss and all the branches have been pruned and wired where necessary. The pruning was severe— leaving only a basic framework upon which to build more dignified branches in years to come.

Ten weeks after planting, all trees in the forest have grown well. Many of the long shots you see here have grown directly from the trunks—a result of the hard pruning that the trees underwent after planting. But there is ample healthy growth on all the existing branches as well.

My new forest on a hillside, after its first trim in late May 2000. All the individual trees are growing well, so I anticipate at least one more serious pruning session this year, maybe two. Every cut is made above a carefully selected bud, so the new shoots will grow in the right direction. From now on, I'll cut out all unwanted buds and shoots as soon as they appear.

there are occasions when three trees appear in a straight line. Now, this doesn't matter a hoot when viewed from the intended angle, and I really don't bother too much about these kinds of "rules." But nothing bugs me more than when I display a tree and all my peers take great pleasure in pointing out the flaws. I'll readjust the offending trees when I next repot.

All trees survived the transplanting and grew vigorously, encouraged by liberal doses of organic fertilizer pellets embedded in the soil. Less than three months later a serious pruning was needed. Not only did the extending shoots need cutting back to carefully selected buds, but the myriad fine adventitious shoots springing from the trunks needed to be cut out. Zelkovas are prolific producers of these shoots, which is great when you reach the refinement stage but a pain during development.

The second flush of growth was as vigorous as the first. By late June the foliage canopy was again dense, so another pruning was needed. More generous feeding and a third conscientious pruning followed during that season.

Although I am keen to reproduce the seasonal changes in ambience that occur beneath the canopy of a natural broad-leaved forest, I also want the composition as a whole to look good. As you should now already realize, I appreciate the winter image far more than the summer one, so achieving tiny leaves is less important to me than developing good branch structure and fine ramification. Although the two do usually go hand in hand.

THE DESIGNER FOREST

The principles of planning the layout of a bonsai forest planting are well published, but the arrangement of the branches is often ignored in the erroneous belief that the relationship between the trunk lines is the only important factor. True, they are important in setting the character of the work, but there is more to it than that:

• If the thickest trunks are to remain thickest, they should carry more foliage than the others. Conversely, the thinnest trunks should carry the least. This may sound obvious, but you'd be amazed at how often this simple fact is ignored.

• To maximize the beauty of both trunks and branches, the "no crossing" rule applies. No branches should grow inward, and no trunk should grow upward through the branches of a neighbor. These statements are based on natural common sense as well as aesthetics. If two trees are growing in close proximity, the apices of the younger and smaller tree will arch outward to reach the light. A smaller tree next to that will do the same, and so on.

• The rule of placing all the thinner trees at the rear is a general one. Adding one or two small trees in the front or to the sides often adds realism.

Junipers

CHINESE JUNIPERS, with their scale foliage pressed tightly to the shoots, are the perfect species group for beginners and experienced artists alike.

Junipers have everything: flexibility, dense foliage, hardiness, resilience and a predictability that is matched by few other species. By carefully manipulating the branches and shoots on a dense juniper, you can create an almost complete bonsai image in a single session.

The most notable feature of Chinese junipers, however, is their natural method of economizing. They shut off water and nutrient supply to certain branches in times of environmental stress or even as a part of the natural aging process. These branches eventually become stripped and bleached by the elements to form bone-colored jins and sharis. Far from indicating that the plant is in poor condition, the appearance of natural jins means that it is behaving exactly as it should.

The opportunity to use the palette of colors offered by the orange-red underbark, the rich green foliage and the bleached deadwood—as well as their malleability cooperation—make Chinese junipers the most sculpturally obliging of all bonsai.

A weathered jin. No juniper would be complete without them.

From ashes to...

THE PHOENIX GRAFT TECHNIQUE
Blaauws juniper (Juniperus media x Blaauwii)

*If you do it,
do it well and,
above all, don't
lie about it.
It's only a
deception if
it is your
intention to
deceive.*

Always use brass staples or screws when working with junipers. Steel—even stainless or coated steel—kills them if allowed to contact the cambium.

THE "WRAPAROUND" is arguably the most controversial of all bonsai techniques. The Japanese call the practice a *tanuki*, implying deception or a cheat. As you can imagine, this technique is frowned upon in Japanese bonsai. On the other hand, American bonsai artist Dan Robinson once coined the memorable phrase "Phoenix Graft," which views the process from an entirely different perspective. The terms *tanuki* and phoenix graft clearly illustrate the difference in attitude that can and does exist—not only between East and West, but also between individual artists.

If you set out to make a *tanuki*—a deception—you will have no respect for your work, so you'll take less care. But if you set out to create a phoenix graft, the implication is that you are embarking on a more noble quest. What could possibly be wrong with combining a magnificent piece of driftwood—nature's art—with the living vigor and enthusiasm of a healthy young plant, to create an object of great dignity and beauty?

The wraparound isn't a shortcut to achieving a "finished" bonsai—far from it! But it is a means of creating a certain type of image when you don't have suitable material or when you have a wonderful piece of driftwood that you simply must use.

There are many so-called foolproof ways to persuade a living trunk to stick to a piece of dead wood. One is to carve a dovetail groove in the driftwood and insert a thin stem. As the stem thickens it becomes trapped and can only continue to grow through the opening of the groove. Once it has reached the outside world, it's supposed to spread sideways and grow flat against the driftwood. Another suggests binding the living stem to the driftwood until, miraculously, it somehow sticks all by itself. I tried these and other techniques and found none that worked satisfactorily. However, amidst the ashes of apparent defeat stood one tree with hidden potential.

In 1986 I had stapled two Blaauws junipers to a beautiful piece of driftwood—weathered roots from a fallen spruce. The plants I used were too thick and impossible to bend, so I carved grooves in the driftwood to accommodate them and fixed them with brass staples. The growth was so strong that the healing edge of the bark grew into the unavoidable gaps between the trunk and the driftwood and eventually threatened to split the trunks away.

I gave up! It remained in a wooden box for six years—the victim of contemptuous neglect in the hope that someone would take pity and take it off my hands. One day, while delivering a particularly intense sales pitch, I began to realize that I wasn't lying. There really was some potential here. The more I studied the tree, the more it became apparent that I was not looking at a failure. The failure was mine—I had failed to see.

I had been regarding the so-called faults as unacceptable and unforgivable. But I had been ignoring the tree's assets: the sweep of the driftwood, the strategically positioned branches, the dense growth close to the trunk. I suddenly realized what the initial training followed by years of routine watering and the occasional feed had produced. Surely, any yamadori pre-

1986: The three original components. I'd stripped the junipers of unwanted branches and soaked the driftwood in brand-name timber preservative (making sure it was a type safe to plants when dry) and treated it with lime sulfur. At its base you can see a pad of car filler paste with wires embedded in it. The idea was that this would help stabilize the assembly in a pot, but that was to cause problems later.

senting that kind of potential would probably have equally serious faults that would require just as much work and ingenuity to resolve.

I took this tree into my workshop in late October 1994, where I worked on it for at least two or three hours every night, considering each move carefully, until early January 1995.

At the outset I decided to aim for the perfect result by disguising all evidence of the fact that this bonsai was a wraparound. To aim for anything less would defeat the purpose. I also made up my mind always to present the finished result as a phoenix graft—a distinct style in itself. If it was good enough, it would eventually gain the same integrity as a natural driftwood bonsai. To lie about it would simply turn it back into a *tanuki*.

Stage one completed. I had no clear idea of the final form this tree would adopt, or how long it would take to achieve it, but realizing that the supple branches would stiffen quickly, I wired them to shape immediately.

GRAFTING THE LIVING TO THE DEAD

Gouge a channel in the driftwood to accommodate the new trunk. Strip the bark from the part of the trunk to be inserted in the channel. Drive brass screws or staples through the thickest parts of the trunk into the driftwood at alternating angles to provide a secure fixing. Where trunks are too thin for stapling, a variety of devices can be used to hold them tight against the driftwood until they set in position.

55

1994. Almost there. I've been working slowly on the design for a couple of weeks, and the image is beginning to emerge. At this point I have to decide whether the apex should be at the top of the main trunk, forming a slanting style, or swing toward the left, stabilizing the design. The beautiful sweep of the apical jins on the driftwood told me that the apex should follow their movement and lean toward the left.

1994: the real work begins

Before beginning to style this tree I spent many long hours wondering how to correct all the faults it presented. Not until I was fully satisfied that I could do this effectively, did I begin work on the design.

Getting the living trunks to fit snugly against the driftwood had proved impossible from the outset and, in places, I had neglected to remove the cambium beneath the bark inside the carved channels in the driftwood. Over the years this had caused new bark to form inside the channels. Also, in some areas there were still large gaps where I had found it necessary to carve away excessive amounts of driftwood just to enable the trunks to make reasonable contact with it throughout its length.

I had to completely remove the bark that had grown into the channels, which was not easy. As I scraped away with a variety of improvised tools, such as a sharpened screwdriver, a bent meat skewer and some odd implement I pirated from a manicure set, I became increasingly angry with myself for not being more conscientious years before.

The problem of a poorly executed assembly was worst at the top, where the living trunk peeled away from the driftwood, leaving a "V"-shaped notch. This looked unnatural and would reveal this bonsai's secret for eternity if not properly attended to. In hindsight, perhaps it would have been better if I had cut the living trunk off at the top and allowed a side shoot to become the new leader. This would have creat-

ed a more pronounced angle that would have been more likely to disguise itself through natural growth.

I filled all these gaps, from top to bottom, with natural-colored exterior wood filler, making sure I forced it as far into the cavities as possible. This time around I wanted good contact between the live and the dead! The filler was smoothed and sanded flush with the driftwood, and shaped so that it just met the newly exposed heartwood of the living trunk exactly at the point where the bark was cut. This would ensure that as the wounds healed, the new bark would eventually roll over the filler and help to hold it in position if it should begin to crack as the driftwood expanded and contracted with changes in the weather. In the fullness of time, the bark should cover the filler completely.

Also, in 1986 I had used car filler paste to form a base to the driftwood. The idea was that this would stop water from soaking into the end grain of the wood, causing it to rot. I also intended to use it to hold heavy wires that would stabilize the contraption in the pot. Nice idea—but I made a serious and fundamental mistake. I failed to attach the plants high enough on the driftwood, which meant that when the surface roots were exposed, so was that unsightly blob of car filler! You can always remedy branches, but roots are much more difficult—in this case impossible. One alternative would have been to layer or graft on a new set of roots, but neither of these techniques is fool-

THE LESSON

The theory behind the *tanuki* technique has thus far been that by stripping bark from the side of the living trunk which meets the driftwood, the healing callus will grow around the driftwood and eventually stick. This would work perfectly with almost all broad-leaved species, as well as larch and most pines—but, ironically, it just doesn't work on junipers!

Junipers are the only species I have encountered that seem never to heal over open wounds *(see picture on page 58)*. Instead, the cut edge remains, or even dies back gradually year by year. This is precisely why sharis are such prominent and persistent features on junipers growing freely in harsh environments.

The repairs

Here the right-hand trunk forked about halfway up and I had to carve away much driftwood to accommodate it. After eight years' growth the branches had thickened a lot but the large gap remained. I filled this with exterior wood filler and shaped it afterward. In time, as the branches and trunk thicken, new bark should grow right over the filler and conceal it completely.

At the top of the main trunk the dead and living parts separated, leaving a "V"-shaped notch, that provided clear evidence of the tree's history. I carved the new jin on the living trunk to a similar size and texture as the jin on the driftwood and filled the gap with exterior wood filler. After shaping and treatment with lime sulfur, the two parts almost appear as one.

Cross section of the trunk of a six- or seven-year-old wild scale-foliage juniper with a shari caused by damage, perhaps by browsing animals or falling rocks.

The edges occasionally attempt to callus over the exposed wood but, inevitably, die back irregularly over the years. The central core of resinous heartwood extends.

As the process is repeated, the sapwood gradually erodes, leaving behind the bleached heartwood. The margins of each year's die-back create the familiar ridged texture. Almost all wild junipers

develop sharis on trunks and branches resulting in a cross section similar to this after many decades, which signal great age. This is the shape to emulate when carving.

The false nebari

The answer to the lack of nebari on the driftwood was to "graft" on another piece of driftwood from the same tree. After very careful matching of grain and much laborious sanding of the cut surfaces, I finally married the two pieces together and fixed them with epoxy resin and concealed brass screws.

The right-hand side of the new nebari was almost perfect from the start, but the left-hand side needed to be drastically reduced in size and shaped to harmonize with its neighbor and with the texture of the trunk.

proof and both invariably leave their tell-tale scars. They are both likely to cause some die-back when the original roots are cut off. Messing with a tree's vascular system is a risky business, especially on junipers, which have a natural tendency to shed branches and develop sharis after stress.

Although the filler could eventually have been carved to shape, it would never adopt the natural texture and color of the driftwood, and lime sulfur had no effect whatsoever—it simply ran off.

If grafting on new living roots wasn't acceptable, perhaps the answer was to "graft" on a set of artificial dead roots? Fortunately I had collected several smaller pieces of driftwood from the same fallen spruce tree, so I selected a piece of similar width to the trunk and with reasonable natural movement that seemed to follow that of the trunk. It was also important to check that the grain would match when the two pieces were fitted together.

I made the joint at an angle, since diagonal lines in any object or design are far less noticeable than horizontal or vertical lines. I emphasized the natural grain for some distance above and below the joint by subtle carving, mainly with a wire brush attachment on a Dremel, to disguise the joint further. The joint can still be seen, but when the wood isn't bone dry, and

Years in a large growing box had allowed the tree to grow rapidly.

Compare the base of the trunk after the initial assembly to its appearance ten years later. See how much the trunk has thickened and how the exposed roots have changed almost beyond recognition due to the change in demand by the branches above. Surprisingly, the scar left by the brass staple is still clearly visible, although it has adopted a natural and unobtrusive appearance.

CARVING TIPS

Electric power tools achieve nothing hand tools can't. They just do it more quickly, enabling the artist to apply his ideas while they are fresh. On the other hand, they encourage the inexperienced to work without consideration, often leading to disastrous results! The best advice is to avoid the very fast-operating tools and bits at first and to take your time. Bonsai take years to develop, so saving a few hours on the carving is neither here nor there.

A wide range of carving bits is available in tool and woodcarving stores in both 1/4 in. (6mm) and 1/8 in. (3mm) shank sizes:

• **Disks and wheels** remove wood at an alarming rate. Some have replaceable teeth and others are rimmed with a section of chain saw. Only for the experienced.

• **Steel cutters are small,** bladed cutters in a variety of shapes that have a tendency to clog when used on unseasoned wood.

• **Tungsten carbide burrs** are minute, very sharp and durable teeth bonded to a variety of shaped bits. Wood is removed easily and smoothly. Clog occasionally.

• **Smoothers** are circular wire brushes and sandpaper flapwheels for a really smooth finish. Wire brushes are also useful for adding subtle texture to fresh wood.

Refining the jins and driftwood

The original jins were smooth, which is fine if the image being created is that of a more compact tree. In this case the image is of a large, majestic tree, so the jins needed to be refined.

When shaping a jin I try to make the carving tell a story. Hollowing out the center creates different bands of texture that make the jin visually lighter and simulates decay, increasing its apparent age. The shape of the top edge implies that scar tissue had "rolled" over the original wound until that, too, had eventually died.

Although the driftwood was old, the grain of woody tissue in roots is such that the surface remains smooth, with just a few hairline cracks. To add an authentic texture, these cracks were exaggerated with a sharp scalpel. More were added, taking care to avoid overkill. Then with the wire brush fitted to my Dremel, I smoothed out the sharp edges and emphasized all the slight undulations, until a more sinuous effect was achieved.

When using power tools such as Dremel or Makita, always wear eye protection. Seemingly harmless wire brushes can cause serious injury as the worn filaments fly in all directions.

lime sulfur has recently been applied, it's only visible on very close inspection.

Continuing development

As soon as the shaping was complete, I commissioned a pot from British potter Bryan Albright. We have a long tradition of top-quality, creative ceramic artists in the United Kingdom and, fortunately, many are now turning their talents to bonsai containers. Most are happy to design a pot for approval, based on photographs and dimensions of the tree. Surprisingly, handmade pots are hardly more expensive than imported Japanese pots. The advantage is that you get the pot you want, not just the nearest you can find from a naturally limited selection at your local nursery. This pot, which Bryan designed himself, is dull purple/red with a coarse, unglazed finish—a perfect match.

By midsummer 1995, the foliage had begun

TOP: June 1995.
As the foliage begins to grow it takes on the appearance of clouds drifting through the towering dead branches. I liked this image very much.

RIGHT: Summer 1996. After only a little more than one season's growth, the foliage has already begun to bulk up. The negative areas between the branches have reduced and the whole image has become more unified. It is softer, somehow, with more horizontal emphasis, and seems to depict a smaller tree. I liked this image too.

to fill in the sparse areas and, as a result, the image was becoming stronger. I had considered how to accelerate this process when wiring the branches. I wired the lateral branches downward from the primary branches and I carefully trimmed the finer shoots to fan-shaped tufts by cutting out all the vigorous central portions. Each tuft was then positioned so it overlapped the one below—like tiles on a roof, but with space between them to allow for growth. Where possible, I laid some of these fans of foliage over the primary and secondary branches to fill in vacant spaces. The whole process was one of distributing foliage as evenly as possible throughout the entire area of the branch.

The system worked—rather too well, if anything! Within one year the clouds had filled in and matured nicely. At this point, summer 1996, the image had just about achieved its peak in terms of balance of foliage and negative areas. Now I had to figure out how to maintain it, and

CONTROL OF JUNIPERS

Scale-foliage junipers produce two types of shoot. Non-extending shoots grow *en masse* but only a very short amount each year. Almost imperceptibly, the tree swells. Extending shoots, which are brighter and plumper, can grow up to 8 in. (20cm) or more in a season.

Pinching growing tips of non-extending shoots keeps the foliage neat. The tree responds by energizing more of the same type of shoot from within the foliage mass.

Extending shoots must be *cut* back to a point where all the remaining laterals on the shoot are the non-extending type.

August 1999.
I have already removed a weak branch growing from the rear on the left. The clouds of foliage have now become far too heavy, giving the tree a brutish air. The lower right-hand branch was misbehaving too—in spite of the fact that it had been tied in position with fine wire for four years, it still insisted on raising itself four or five degrees.

I found trying to maintain a neat, more delicate foliage silhouette on the rigid branch framework to be frustrating. Junipers are naturally fuller, more rounded trees than the pines and larches upon which I had based this design.

I didn't like this image at all, so a rethink was clearly necessary.

One branch toward the rear of the tree had never recovered from the initial styling and had become even weaker since. The foliage was gray and lacklustre, and there were some patches where the foliage had died. There was no apparent reason for this within the branch itself— no infestations of spider mites, no colonies of scale insects, no bark fractures. I traced the living vein down toward the roots...

...until I found the cause. There was one branch below the weak one, and below that the living vein was very thin, where I had been over-ambitious in creating a jin. This vein was clearly incapable of sustaining both branches above it, and the first one was stealing the lion's share of water and nutrients. My only option was to remove the weakest branch, thereby ensuring the continued health of the strongest.

In the end, I jinned the weakest branch (on the right) and another higher up that was also not performing too well. The effect achieved when creating new shari and jins around older ones can be pleasing once the wood has weathered. It creates a texture that is difficult to imitate and tells a little of the history of the tree.

in trying to do so I discovered that the branch design I had used was not really appropriate for scale-foliage junipers. Pines, larch and needle junipers are ideally suited to this horizontal emphasis in their branches because they have discernible individual shoots that can be controlled and repositioned with ease. But scale-foliage junipers have so many growing shoots, this is simply not possible. The foliage seems to expand *en masse*, like an inflating balloon.

By summer 1998, the branches had developed a square-shouldered appearance, so I needed to rethink my design and create a more appropriate branch structure, allowing for more rounded foliage masses that would be easier to maintain.

There was another problem: one branch, toward the rear on the left, was very weak and suffering some die-back of inner shoots. I traced the cause to some rather overambitious shari-making on part of the secondary trunk that supported this branch. I hadn't left enough living tissue to sustain the two branches above the shari, and the dying branch was the uppermost. Clearly the lower one was increasingly stealing its nutrition as the foliage expanded.

There was no question—the weak branch had to go, and the sooner the better! Rather than cut it off, I retained it as a jin. Sometimes an uncomfortable or too-powerful negative area can be subtly subdued with a delicate jin, whereas a foliage-bearing branch would be overkill. Similarly, converting a branch to a jin can often lighten a heavily designed tree without altering its overall visual balance.

During July 1998 I redesigned the branch structure, converting two more to jins and removing another entirely. The primary and secondary branches were thick and fairly short, making them very difficult to bend without risking damage. It was only possible to move them slightly to redirect the tertiary branches and shoots. Shoots that had originally been laid horizontally over the branch were raised as far as possible and the shoots below were raised to a progressively lesser degree as they proceeded outward. I shortened all branches to keep a compact shape.

The final result is a much fuller, more mature image—that of a larger tree, and one that should be far easier to maintain. But one thing is inevitable—in a few years' time it will change again.

Blaauws juniper—tanuki

Summer 1999

27 inches (68cm) high; 25 inches (62cm) wide.
Pot commissioned from Bryan Albright

Buried treasure

RAFT STYLE WITH A DIFFERENCE

Juniperus chinensis "sargentii" (Shimpaku juniper)

Once in a while a tree comes along that has virtually no appeal at first sight but has one special feature. Sometimes this might be easily overlooked.

THIS IS THE story of a shimpaku juniper (*Juniperus chinensis "sargentii"*), about 34 inches (85cm) tall, which was grown in Japan and exported as raw material—an increasingly common practice these days. When I acquired it, the tree was brimming with health and growing vigorously, although the inner foliage and some of the smaller branches were beginning to die because of the extremely dense growth, which was to be expected.

The trunk has a fairly attractive curve at the base where it sweeps up from the ground, but from there on up it is far less inspiring. All in all, it was a pretty mundane, run-of-the-mill kind of bush. So why did I choose this plant to work on at all?

I am often confronted with material that is, at first sight, uninspiring, but there is usually some feature that can be utilized to make the result unique and exciting. In the case of this juniper, I found just such a feature in the very low branch emerging just above ground level on the right and slightly toward the rear. This one branch, seemingly insignificant, was to prove

Juvenile foliage consists of needlelike leaves that usually occur in groups of three and stand almost at right angles from the shoot.

Adult foliage consists of scales that are pressed tightly to the shoot, giving it a cordlike appearance.

JUNIPER FOLIAGE

Scale-leaved junipers generally have two types of foliage, depending on the growth phase that the plant, or a particular part of the plant, is experiencing at the time. Juvenile growth occurs when the plant is either in its infancy or when it has been forced into infantile behavior by some form of maltreatment. This might be indelicate transplanting, over-enthusiastic pruning or a diet too rich in nitrates. It can also appear after natural environmental stress such as drought or disease.

Under normal circumstances, junipers resume production of adult foliage within a single season—two at most. Normal circumstances are moderate feeding and watering, no root disturbance and gentle but regular shoot pinching. If you treat a juniper in the juvenile phase gently but it refuses to revert to the adult phase, something is definitely amiss, and it's probably in the roots.

the key element in the design concept of this bonsai. Small details like this are normally totally overlooked in the search for a more total solution to the problem at hand. But when considering possible designs for any tree, it's essential to look at every single detail carefully. You never know when you might find something, some tiny feature, upon which the entire design concept can be built.

What had to be done with the trunk and main branches was almost routine: cut away the lower branches and wire down the upper ones. Of course there was some thought necessary, but nothing to agonize over. The result would be a reasonable bonsai image, but nothing special. If anything, it would be a little boring, uninspired and uninspiring. That's where the little low branch came in....

Over 70% of the branches were discarded, almost all from the lower part of the trunk. There was the usual cluster of potential apices where the trunk forked into three at the top, so two of these went as well. Before wiring the main branches, I wrapped the thicker ones with raffia to protect them against splitting while being bent. Positioning the branches and foliage was almost routine.

Now you'll see the significance of the low branch. It was very low on the trunk—more or

Straight from the delivery truck, this uninspiring juniper seems more suited to the shrub border than a bonsai pot.

JUNIPER SHOOTS

There are the normal, well-behaved shoots that all grow at the same steady pace and create wonderful dense, soft, green clouds.

Then there are the runts, darker green, almost gray sometimes, and very thin. These are found in the inner parts, where they're starved of light and fresh air. Although they can live for years, they never seem to gain strength, even after being exposed to the sun and air. Instead, new, more vigorous shoots spring from their bases.

Finally there are the hotheads, the lighter green, fatter shoots that bolt from within the well-behaved shoots and extend rapidly. These are the shoots that the plant has decided (or thinks it has decided) are going to be future branches.

The picture shows juniper shoots in their various guises. From top to bottom: the runts, the hotheads and the well-behaved shoots.

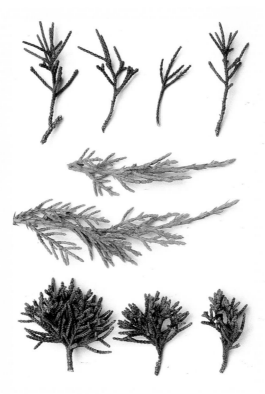

PREPARING JUNIPERS FOR WIRING

The secret of success lies in the careful preparation of both tree and artist. As the artist prepares the tree, their relationship becomes more intimate. They learn to cooperate, accepting each other's faults and limitations and working together as a team.

A typical section of virgin branch on a shimpaku juniper. Before wiring, it has to be carefully prepared.

All the unwanted foliage and shoots have now been removed. The outer foliage has also been separated into individual tufts, borne at the tips of last year's shoots.

Fine wiring should be continued right up to the base of every tuft of foliage, and should end in a loose loop. This makes it possible to bend all the tufts slightly upward, giving the foliage a much fuller appearance and adding visual bulk to the now sparse branches.

Chinese junipers—in fact virtually all scale-foliage junipers—are a joy to wire. Their flexibility enables you to position the branches and shoots wherever you desire, and their dense ramification can produce an almost "finished" image at the first attempt. Before wiring, however, it's essential to prepare the branches by cleaning the bark and removing all the inappropriate growth.

First, All the loose and flaky bark on the thicker branches should be brushed off with a soft brass wire brush. If you don't have a suitable brush, sandpaper will do, but it's a trickier operation. Even smaller branchlets that are only two or three years old should be cleaned if possible. Many branches will have small raised lenticels that reveal the tree's immaturity and interfere with wiring. These can be smoothed gently with sandpaper, taking care not to remove the surrounding tissue. The small areas of exposed cambium heal within a couple of days and the tree suffers no harm.

Second, all the runts must be stripped off. This is easy because they are weakly attached and come away with little resistance.

Third, small shoots growing from the forks between branches or shoots must go. These would interfere with the wiring and, if allowed to grow, would also clutter the outer areas, making maintenance more awkward.

Fourth, the hotheads must be cut back to well-behaved laterals. The only time you leave a hothead unpruned is when you want to extend a branch. In this case, it should remain unwired. Extending branches thicken rapidly, so wire marks are a serious risk.

Finally, the remaining foliage must be further thinned to separate it into individual tufts at the tips of last year's growth. This overall thinning will induce new, strong replacement growth.

Naturally, you'll wire all the fine shoots, right up to the base of each tuft—right? Remember to end each wire in a loop, so you can bend each tuft to face upward. This way, the clouds of foliage appear more mature and the result looks less like a freshly wired tree.

THINNING JUNIPERS

Junipers require constant pinching throughout the growing season. They can swell imperceptibly as all the well-behaved shoots extend in unison, and this must be controlled. Before wiring, a more thorough and comprehensive session is needed. The approach differs according to the type of foliage or shoot you are dealing with.

All juvenile foliage

Cut with sharp shears. Only current season's shoots will respond to cutting by sprouting new lateral shoots. Older shoots will abort after cutting, and this will only encourage more juvenile growth. Cut current season's growth sparingly—little and often. Cut out completely any dead or clearly dying shoots. Don't attempt to train a tree that is in juvenile phase, because most of what you see will be entirely different in a year's time.

Runts

These should be cut off and discarded. Don't cut into the parent branch, but leave the little brown sheath at the base of the shoot intact. This preserves the area where more useful vigorous shoots are likely to appear, and you'll need those in a few years.

Hotheads

Turn your back for five minutes and you can bet there'll be another one popping up somewhere! They mingle with the crowd until they think you're not looking and suddenly bolt for it! They must also be cut out completely. Cut back to a pair of healthy laterals, well within the foliage mass.

Well-behaved shoots

These you can pinch in the time-honored way—grip a fan of shoots between thumb and forefinger of one hand and pull off the ends with the other. The broken tips sometimes turn brown in the sun. Pulling them off, rather than breaking them, helps prevent this. So does a period of semi-shade and regular spraying. Once a year, you should thin out some of the older, stouter green shoots to let more delicate ones through.

less at the same level as the nebari on the opposite side of the trunk. It was also around the same thickness as the nebari. In fact, if I bent the branch down into the soil, it actually became nebari. Neat! But that's not the end of it. I pinned the branch into the soil and then bent it up again about six inches (15cm) to the right of the trunk and slightly toward the rear. I bent it at the point where it forked into two secondary branches. By positioning these with wire they became two tiny, distant trunks.

In close-up you can see the attention paid to the wiring and shaping of the secondary trees. It's important to work at such detail on secondary trees because they must always be kept delicate and open, and they need to be properly structured for this purpose from the outset. If I ever allow them to become too dense, they will begin to look like shrubs at the base of the main tree and not like trees of a similar size and shape far in the distance.

Of course the inclination of the soil surface was not right. I had tilted the pot quite a bit to add some visual energy to the main trunk line, and the design was based on an imaginary horizontal plane of soil. The secondary trees would also be more realistically presented if the soil

The low branch I discovered lurking beneath the dense foliage. This was to become the key to the whole design.

This was one of the rare occasions when I have worked on a tree within a few weeks of acquiring it. Normally I would wait a few years to make sure the tree is healthy and I am confident in my plans. But, in this case, I had no concerns about either. I bought the tree in May 1997. By the end of June I had completed the initial training.

I call this a raft planting because I guess that's what it is, even though the trunk is still upright. It's not a clump, and it's not root-connected, so what else can it be?

THE METAMORPHOSIS

After stripping away some of the lower branches, I could consider the planting angle. Leaning the tree toward the right and slightly forward enhanced the limited movement of the trunk.

After removing a few more branches and turning the pruned branch stubs into jins, I began to wire the main branches so that they would sweep downward. You can see the point where the trunk splits into three at the apex.

level was raised a little on the right. However, it was a little too late in the season to risk repotting. Even though the tree was certainly strong enough to withstand the root disturbance, there seemed little point in rushing the job. After all, it would be several years before the juniper was developed enough to display—even on the classy benches in my own garden. Besides, I didn't have a suitable pot!

My first instinct was to plant the composition on a slab of some sort. This would, I thought, reinforce the all-important horizontal axis I needed to establish as a base for the design. Having had some success with making natural-looking concrete slabs (*see page 46*), I decided to devote a week during the following

winter to making a custom-designed slab for my new raft. The result wasn't bad at all—a nice slab, good thickness, realistic texture, and a clever little split that I had introduced in the front profile seemed to suit the gentle sweep of the trunks perfectly.

I introduced the tree to the slab in late spring of 1998. However, after combing out the old, *akadama* (japanese bonsai soil) from the root ball, the roots weren't substantial enough to support the tree at my chosen angle, especially since I had pruned away almost all the heavy roots on the left-hand side (leaving enough fine root on the visible nebari to ensure its survival). I needed to find a way to support the tree. Rather than drill holes in my nice new slab, I

With as many branches to choose from as this plant offered me, I had no trouble arranging them into a more or less completed image. It's a little too open, but that state isn't going to last for long on any juniper!

The "pièce de résistance"—the low branch has now been pinned to the soil and trained to represent two distant trees. Note the harmony between the three trunk lines.

used string to hold the tree at the desired angle.

Now, here's something you should never do. I used a mycorrhiza inoculant—no bad thing in itself—but the product contained that awful water-retaining gel that the chemical conglomerates seem intent on forcing upon the unsuspecting horticultural world. Five minutes after I finished watering the newly replanted juniper, I noticed that the gel had expanded and the soil had risen to almost double its original level. The strings were pulled so tight that, as the expanding soil pushed the tree upward, one of the strings snapped and the tree toppled.... Clearly something those big brains didn't take into account when they invented the stuff! Take my advice, and steer clear of water-retaining gel.

I had to introduce considerable detail into the small secondary trees in order to make them realistic.

BELOW: Summer 1998. Once planted on its custom-made slab, I thought the composition would be complete, but something wasn't quite right. The slab didn't allow me to emphasize the horizontal axis that this composition needed.

RIGHT: This simple wire clip enabled me to adjust the tension of the guy strings to accommodate the expansion and contraction of the dreadful water-retaining gel that I had so stupidly included in the soil.

I didn't want to disturb the poor roots any more than I had done already, so replacing all the soil was out of the question. In the end, I replaced only the outer covering of soil and devised a simple way to adjust the tension of my guy strings as the moisture content of the soil caused it to expand and contract. Fortunately, we had a dry summer that year! By early August the roots had bonded the soil into one mass and I was able to keep the guy strings permanently loosened, but with just enough tension to prevent the tree from toppling in the wind.

It was around that time that I began to question the suitability of the slab. Immediately after training, when the foliage was thin, the slab seemed appropriate—especially when contrasted with the heavy mica training pot. But now, with greater bulk in all three trees, the composition seemed to have lost its way. (The featureless, uniform, unmossed profile of the soil didn't help much either, but moss just won't grow on rolling stones or constantly expanding and contracting soil—but let's not go there again...!) The composition needed a strong horizontal axis and a flat soil surface to establish a sense of distance between the main tree and the two secondary trees. On a slab this size, a really flat soil surface is not possible.

I lived with the slab for another year, not really giving much consideration to finding an alternative container. Then, in spring 2000, I was pruning an elm group when I thought to myself: "This would look better on a slab—wish I had one...." Aha! I did have one. It's strange how these connections are made but, after I swapped the containers, the elm forest did look better on the slab. The oval pot from Walsall Studio provided the juniper raft with all the horizontal emphasis it could wish for.

By midsummer 2000, the image had just about arrived. It could be pinched and trimmed for another two or three years without passing its prime. But soon after that, it will need to be thoroughly cleaned of extraneous shoots, relieved of thick outer sub-branches and totally rewired. With any composition that uses implied distance as a key component, space has just as important a role to play as mass. At some future point, I suspect that a few branches could be pruned out and the foliage replaced by repositioning other branches. No matter how final you think the image might be, it's always only temporary.

Pot swap. I robbed an elm group of its pot and tried the juniper in it. Bingo! The elm group looks pretty neat on the slab, too!

Shimpaku juniper—raft

Summer 2000

**32 inches (80cm) high; 24 inches (60cm) wide.
Pot by Walsall Studio**

Back to basics

SHOHIN JUNIPER FROM CUTTINGS
Juniperus chinensis 'sargentii'

If you think shohin, or miniature bonsai, are for novices or the faint-hearted, try making one yourself. You'll change your mind as sure as night follows day.

MOST SHIMPAKU juniper bonsai are started in Japan and imported to the West. They're produced in very large numbers to a formula—as often as not with a spiraling trunk and tastefully radiating branches. At first sight they all look pretty good, if somewhat similar. But after a while, you begin to realize that they are really too artificial, as if they are the Eastern concept of what will satisfy Western demand. Besides, where's the challenge in a plant on which all the important decisions have already been made?

Back in 1981, when I harbored dreams of running my own bonsai nursery, I took dozens of cuttings from a garden center shimpaku bush. My intention was to grow them all on and sell them as raw material in years to come. It didn't take long before I decided that there just weren't enough days in the week to make good bonsai for myself and to nurture hundreds of bad ones for someone else. I abandoned the idea and gave all but five plants away.

Two are still untrained—growing in large tubs, with the most interesting parts currently being air-layered. One is recovering from a bad attack of spider mite that it contracted while it was lurking at the back of my overcrowded border, and I swapped another for a tasty yamadori hawthorn. The remaining one has now been put to good use.

PROPAGATING JUNIPER CUTTINGS

A heel cutting of last year's growth.

Chinese junipers are best rooted from cuttings taken in early summer. In warmer areas you can propagate them a little earlier, as soon as the extending shoots become brighter in color and noticeably plumper.

Take cuttings of last year's shoots by pulling them away from the parent branch, together with a heel of older bark. This happens quite naturally, so there's no special technique involved. Trim the heel with a sharp blade to remove loose material.

Dip the cuttings in rooting hormone if you wish (I never bother) and insert them into a propagating tray containing 50% sand, 20% peat and 30% chopped, fresh sphagnum moss.

Water thoroughly with a solution of copper fungicide to prevent rotting in the confinement of the propagator, and place the lid over the tray, with the ventilation half open. Keep the tray in semi-shade until the cuttings have started new growth, which may be quite some time. Junipers have an uncanny ability to live on their own juices for a remarkably long time. A juniper that is "root dead" can appear to be alive for well over a year. Your cuttings may take up to two years to root, so don't think that just because they are still green after six months, they have rooted. You can only be certain when you see vigorous extending shoots.

Waste not, want not...

I grew these five junipers in my vegetable plot, waiting for the trunks and main limbs to become thicker, and for the angular, pruning-induced directional changes to become smooth and sinuous. Progress was slowed by moving house in 1989, which meant that I had to lift them and plant them in containers for a year before returning them to the ground. But I was impatient to work on them, so I kept one of them back, and planted it in an even smaller container (a discarded washbowl—well, I had just taken on a new mortgage!). Rather than keeping back the one with the most potential, I opted for the worst. Good young material becomes even better older material. Bad young material can always be rebuilt—almost from the ground up, if necessary.

Junipers take a few years to settle back into regular adult growth after drastic root reduction, so my enthusiasm to begin work was frustrated for a while. By early summer 1992, the tree had regained its composure—so, for the first time, I seriously considered what to do with it. The first problem to address was the slingshot trunk—the very reason I picked this plant in the first place. Second, both trunks were fairly boring, having a slight curve at best. Third, the branches were long, straight and unramified.

My solution to the first problem was to eliminate it by air-layering the smallest trunk.

PREPARATION IN THE GROUND

If you grow junipers in the ground to gain bulk, there are a some points to bear in mind.

You don't want a short, heavy trunk with long, straight branches, but if you're not careful, that's what you'll get. Do some initial shaping of the trunk section before allowing free growth, either by pruning or with ties. Wire is always risky in open ground—many a juniper has wire permanently embedded in the trunk through such folly.

Every year, cut back all the long, straight upper branches to allow light and air to reach the weaker inner foliage. If you don't do this, the inner foliage will die and you will spend a long time trying to regain it.

Every three or four years, it's worth lifting the bush in spring and cutting the heaviest roots back hard.

When growing juniper material in the ground, the upper branches must be cut back hard to allow light and air to reach the weak inner shoots. These are the shoots that will probably form the future branches.

My little homegrown juniper. Without the extraneous foliage, the true horror of the slingshot trunk was revealed.

Spring 1992. Being a penny-pinching miser, I decided to air-layer the unwanted trunk. I just didn't have the heart to throw away something I had spent the last decade or so growing.

Junipers air-layer readily, often producing a mass of vigorous roots within six to eight weeks.

That would come in handy later. By late August the air-layer had taken well so I severed it and potted it up, placing it in the shade to recover.

My solution to the second and third problems was similar. I peeled a frighteningly large shari on the trunk, right down to soil level, and over half the circumference in some places. I picked one branch, which was growing toward the center of the original plant, and kept that as the only living part with which to work. That, too, was almost entirely eliminated when I cut it back to the first two laterals. Needless to say, the poor little juniper responded to such treatment

with a prolific flush of juvenile foliage. I had to wait a further two years before I could begin training. It's ironic that it was impatience that got me into this in the first place, and my impatience had now forced me to play the waiting game.

I now realize that I began training this tree much too early in its development. Unlike deciduous bonsai, junipers aren't easy to build branch-by-branch. It's far better to wait until the material becomes dense and compact under a consistent regime of good horticulture, occasional branch removal and regular pinching. Then you will be able to make the tree without the need for heavy reduction pruning, thus avoiding that dreadful juvenile nonsense.

Meanwhile...

In southern England, Chinese junipers continue growing right through winter in a polytunnel, or hoophouse, which is where I kept the air-layer I had taken. After only one year it had established itself on its new set of roots. By late spring 1994 it was strong enough to withstand the imminent onslaught. Having made the mistake of beginning training too soon on the parent plant, I went ahead and made the same mistake on this one!

I'd just acquired a Dremel power tool with a set of woodcarving bits. Anyone who has one of these beauties will understand exactly why I rushed out and pretended to be Masahiko Kimura for an hour or two. I went berserk with this thing! Off came the top of the trunk, and great fissures appeared in its naked side. In went the tiniest carving bit to etch a tale of storm and tempest in the yielding heartwood. Timber turned brown, then black, as the bit heated up under my frantic demands; smoke began to make my eyes sting, and the kitchen was beginning to smell.... I had a ball!

The result, however, was just the tiniest bit overcooked for such a small tree. Something more subtle would have suited the slanting or windswept tree this plant seemed to suggest. I have a maxim I follow when confronted with such an aberration: "Use it." If the driftwood—or any other feature—is too prominent, make it the focus of the design.

Since I'd removed the top of the trunk, I couldn't go up—so I had to go down. By tilting the plant a little, and lowering the soil level, I

THE FIRST TREE

Spring 1993. The only way to introduce interest and perceived movement in the otherwise featureless trunk was to make a large shari on one side.

Summer 1994. After repotting, the poor, battered juniper grew well enough for me to apply some initial wiring. At this stage, the foliage was still juvenile.

Summer 1995. I had wired this long-suffering plant for a second and a third time and worked on the dead wood with my Dremel power-carving tool.

Spring 1999. I had learned my lesson, and left the tree alone to build up strength before repotting into an antique Japanese container. However, the long branch on the lower right seemed to pull the tree off balance. The image didn't need to be as expansive as this.

Summer 1999. Without the offending branch, the image becomes more compact, better balanced and visually stable. It was also horticulturally easier.

Fall 1999. The foliage had filled out beautifully. There were still small patches of juvenile growth, but nothing that couldn't be removed. At this stage, the discipline changes from one of rapid development to one of slow, steady improvement.

THE SECOND TREE

1994. Flushed with the euphoria of having acquired a new Dremel power-carving tool, I attacked the layered trunk without mercy. Oh, well, we all make mistakes!

Spring 1995. I replanted the tree at a different angle, to reveal some heavy roots. Those on the left were carved to continue the shari.

Summer 1995. The confines of a small pot had forced the tree back into adult phase, for which I was grateful. However, the exposed "Chinese-style" roots looked like an alien creature stuck in a bowl of treacle, for which I was not grateful.

Fall 1995. Yet more changes of mind.... By tilting the plant even further to the right, I could bury the alien's legs and use the lonely branch to begin training a neat little cascade.

Fall 1997. After two years of unhindered growth, my cascade was looking good. The dead alien's legs had by now been jinned and were hanging over the back of the pot, out of sight.

Fall 1997. From the rear, the jinned roots are a dominant feature and add excitement and energy to the overall design. Come to think of it, the original carving looks pretty good from this side also.

SCALE-FOLIAGE JUNIPER VARIETIES

SHIMPAKU (Chinese juniper)—*Juniperus sargentii*

This is the classic Japanese juniper and probably the best. The foliage is rich bright green when young and slightly darker when mature. In harsh winters, the foliage may temporarily become bronze. Shoots are compact and rounded, forking prolifically. The bark on wild plants is dark chestnut brown, peeling when old, occasionally developing a slightly corky texture.

BLAAUWS JUNIPER—*Juniperus media 'Blaauwii'*

A chunkier, more vigorous plant than shimpaku with fatter shoots and foliage that has a distinct blue-gray tint. Tolerates drought. Although more linear in habit than shimpaku when growing freely, it is equally, if not more, dense when regularly pinched. The bark is similar to shimpaku, if sometimes a little more orange.

SABINA (Europe)—*Juniperus sabina*

Very similar in color to shimpaku but with finer, more wiry shoots that are not so willing to fork unless encouraged to do so by constant pinching. The bark is virtually identical to shimpaku. Once established, sabinas rival their eastern cousins in all aspects.

SAN JOSE (North America)—*Juniperus chinensis 'san jose'*

San Jose, Californian and Hollywood junipers develop thicker bark with good character. Although it is possible to peel this away to reveal the orange-red underbark, it would be a travesty and, in my view, should not be done. All the North American junipers have a singular reluctance to produce uniformly adult foliage. No matter how settled they are in their growth, there will always be a disconcerting amount of juvenile foliage. Rather than waste time in a futile attempt to prevent this, cut out all the adult foliage and work only with the juvenile.

GOLDEN JUNIPER—various garden species

Countless ornamental varieties of scale-foliage junipers have been developed, many with attractive golden or yellow foliage, especially in spring and early summer. Avoid these like the plague! They are all weak growers and prone to all manner of infirmities. They respond poorly to pruning and wiring and, frankly, look sick.

was able to expose carvable roots. That certainly gave the shari a life of its own! At least, since there was more of it, the intense detail didn't seem so out of place. The rest of the tree did, though!

The one and only branch I retained was too thick and short to bend effectively. Besides, now that I'd demolished the trunk, there was precious little to anchor wire to. And then there were those odd-looking roots. They made the tree look like an alien creature trying to extricate itself from a bowl of treacle. I decided to tilt the tree even further, so I could bury the roots. This meant that a cascade style was the way to go, so I wired the pitifully sparse branches accordingly. I also made a spiral shari on the main limb, in order to imply movement in years to come.

Back at the first tree...

I fiddled away for a few years, wiring, pruning, rewiring. My constant attempts to organize and control the growth as I had done on my shohin elm (see page 14) only served to prolong the period of juvenile growth and retard progress. It wasn't until late 1995 that I realized what I was doing wrong. For the next four years I let the tree grow as it pleased, only cutting back the occasional overextending shoot. But before doing so, I did use the trusty Dremel to shape the deadwood. This time, I did learn my lesson, and made sue I carved rather more subtle shapes and textures.

In spring 1999 it was sufficiently developed to warrant a decent pot. It wasn't quite there yet, but a smaller container would help compact the growth and make working on the tree a lot more pleasurable. I loved the combination of the old Japanese pot, the nebari and the trunk line, but the tree itself seemed a little too heavy now—and way off balance. The uniformly composed pot and trunk couldn't visually support that long tumbling branch on the right. In fact, there were two branches too many. As soon as I had amputated the two lowest branches, on the right, the balance was almost restored. A little more width, a little less on top....

I may have arrived at the end result via a rather circuitous and masochistic route, but it was worth the effort. This little shohin juniper continues to improve year after year. The shari and live vein are now becoming "naturalized," and the compact foliage has settled into adult

phase—allowing me to begin more precise definition of the different elements within the overall canopy.

And the cascade...?

When I next looked at the roots, in 1997, the alien's legs I had buried were dead—perhaps they were already dead when I buried them. The heartwood was still intact, but the sapwood had begun to decay. Apart from this, I was reasonably satisfied with the way the tree was progressing. It needed thinning and a little internal restructuring, but otherwise it was doing fine. I thought what a neat idea it would be to jin the dead roots and allow them to hang over the back of the pot just for fun. This also let me use a rather nice Tokaname pot that was previously too small.

I always like to make my bonsai as three-dimensional as possible, paying as much attention to perfecting the sides and back as I do to the front. I think that using tricks like contorting a back branch to function as a side branch, or as an apex, is cheating and lacks integrity. Sometimes my approach pays dividends. There I was, admiring the weird hanging jinned roots at the back, when it dawned on me that, for the second time in my bonsai incarnation, the back was better than the front! The original carving now had direction and power. It loomed overhead ominously. The jinned roots still looked like an alien's legs, but this time the creature was leaping into space from a cliff-top. This I liked—a lot.

Like its sister, this juniper has now settled comfortably into adulthood, and continues its program of steady refinement. It's been a long haul—eighteen years—and I've learned a lot of lessons (some of them at least twice!), but for a powerful little cascade shohin juniper like this, I'd do it all again.

Epilogue

Since these two bonsai were developed in parallel, both sections of the same parent plant, I thought it would be more appropriate to present them as a pair in their final pin-up photograph. Compare the two sisters with the picture of the original plant on page 73 and you'll see that, sometimes, starting from scratch can bring rich rewards.

There usually is plenty of time where bonsai are concerned. Why bother, for example, carrying out detailed carving on a shari in one session, or before you have fully considered your approach, when the rest of the tree will take several years to mature? Why not consider your actions for three or four years first and be sure to get it right?

Shimpaku juniper—shohin

Summer 2000

Informal: 6.5 inches (18cm) high; 5.5 inches (14cm) wide.
Antique Japanese container

Cascade: 8 inches (20cm) high; 4.5 inches (12cm) wide.
Tokaname container

A link in the chain

RESTYLING A FAMILIAR CASCADE

Juniperus chinensis sargentii (Shimpaku juniper)

When a bonsai changes hands, its new custodian imposes his own changes— sometimes subtle, at other times more drastic.

SOME YEARS AGO I came across an odd-look-ing cascade shimpaku juniper. It had two curly trunk lines and pompons of foliage at the end of equally curly branches. It was certainly unusual, although I had seen a few of this style before in various nurseries and collections and I knew that a limited batch of them was produced in Japan about thirty years ago. Something about the trunk lines of this one seemed famil-iar to me. I asked all the other owners of similar trees that I could recall, and they all still had

theirs. I shrugged my shoulders and put it on the training bench.

It wasn't in particularly good shape. The foliage was dry and beginning to turn yellow at the tips. The previous owner had decided that it was too dense and, instead of thinning the outer foliage, he had cut off several of the main branches and most of the laterals on the remain-ing branches. Hence the pompons! Pompons is an apt description—dense round blobs of fluffy foliage. There were no shoots or fine sub-

Plate 53. The tree was so completely over- ... greenhouse a... soluti... for the ...

Pla sum

One spring afternoon, a couple of years after I had acquired this juniper, an Australian bon-sai friend paid me a visit. He was rummaging around the training benches, when he let out a yell. "Strewth! I know this tree." I told him that it was familiar to me, too, but I couldn't think why. He strode off to my workshop and emerged with a copy of Peter Adams's *Art of Bonsai* open at page 132. At first I didn't believe that the scruffy piece of material in the book was the same as the scruffy piece of material in my garden, but there were some aspects that were disturbingly similar. I wasn't able to contact the previous owner of my tree, but I did know who had originally acquired the tree pictured in the book. A few phone calls later, and I was convinced. It was the same tree.

It had changed considerably over the years under the various owners. Each of them had their own ideas and had tried to impose them on this itinerant juniper. Now it was my turn....

branches long enough to train—everything was short and stubby. First, I had to nurse this baby back to health and then grow on some longer, trainable shoots from any adventitious growth that appeared.

The root of the matter

As is the case with so many established bonsai—junipers especially, for some reason—this one had a solid core of very old, hard, claylike soil within the root mass. Only the outer inch (25mm) or so had been raked away at each repotting. The hard core couldn't possibly contain any functioning feeder roots, neither was it particularly hospitable to older lignified roots. The peak of this core could clearly be seen on the surface around the nebari, and it didn't take much excavating to discover the full extent of the problem. It was early May when I acquired the tree, and by late May it had deteriorated. It was living on the inch-thick shell of slightly fresher soil around the outside of the solid core, and this, clearly, wasn't enough. Emergency repotting....

It's normally all right to repot Chinese junipers right up until early summer, so I wasn't too nervous about dealing with this one. On the other hand, it was clearly not well, so I had to be very careful. I used a hose with the narrow jet nozzle to wash away as much of the block of old, hard soil as possible, leaving only a little that was wedged in and around the nebari. This was as hard as concrete and will take several more sessions to remove. I used a very loose, water-retentive soil containing Akadama, grit, calcined clay and a generous helping of chopped, fresh sphagnum moss. The latter works magic on most ailing trees, especially Chinese junipers.

The temporary pot I used was a handmade "eggshell" pot which I thought may eventually suit the tree. In the end, I decided the pot was far too heavy visually. It was rather clumsy in its design and it didn't allow the tree the dignity and delicacy that its relatively thin, linear trunks demanded. However, it served its purpose and after one season of almost zero growth, while the tree recovered from whatever had been ailing it, my juniper began to grow with a vengeance. Two years later it was begging me to work on it.

The same tree exhibited at the British national convention in 1989. The foliage masses are too remote from each other, and the design has no unity.

1994, five years later, there had been very little development. One thing has now become obvious, though. The lowest branches are already beginning to weaken.

Although I had established roughly what I had in mind for the design, I still found it difficult to settle on the best side. In a rush of lateral thinking, I realized that if I couldn't solve the problem, I could eliminate it by not deciding on a front. If all the angles look good, why not use them all?

The usual bulbous foliage "clouds" that old junipers display would, in my view, be too heavy and ponderous for a tree with such light and graceful trunks. They would also be incongruous with the spirit of cascading trees, which live in environments where such lush growth is not possible. I like my bonsai to look like trees, to have some credible (if imaginary) natural his-

On closer inspection of the base of the trunks, I realized that there were actually two separate plants that had been crammed together when very young. They showed no sign of self-grafting, so each was in competition with the other. This made the removal of the old, hard soil even more important.

tory, at least. I'm not interested in just making pretty shapes. If this was to look like a credible image of a tree, the design of the foliage had to reflect the environmental influences that could induce such chaotic trunk and branch lines. I saw the trunk and branch configurations like the eddies that occur when a strong wind blows through a city center (or a mountain ravine?). There is an overriding direction to the wind, but things that get caught by it flutter in all directions, like panic-stricken chickens.

Until this moment, this tree had no clear direction, in spite of the exciting, vigorous movement in the trunk and branches—all that energy and nowhere to go!

Okay, I had now settled on the parameters of the design. I had to introduce some visual dynamic that looked good from all sides and presented a credible treelike image. Right from the start I realized that the wildness of the branches needed to be organized into clearly defined areas with spaces between—positive and negative zones that harmonized with the tumbling curves of the trunks. Previous owners had tried to make the tree fit a stereotypical bonsai image, rather than letting the bonsai become a tree.

Eventually, I tired of forever propping up the unsuitable and unstable eggshell pot, and replanted the tree in a rather undignified but more practical plastic flowerpot.

Above: 1997. After spending a couple of years recovering from its former neglect, the juniper was growing nicely. The previous owner had altered the planting angle to make more of a windswept style than a cascade. I disapproved.

Spring 1997. There were so many possible inclinations, the problem of finding the best one was perplexing.

I spent many a long evening trying to decide. Finally I settled on the inclination illustrated here.

The design process

When I work on projects such as this, I try to empathize with the tree whose image I want to present through the medium of bonsai. If I'm dealing with an ancient lowland tree, I try to imagine the smell of decaying wood and wet grass; I play valley-type music on my stereo; and I take a walk in the old woods that run across the foot of my garden. If I'm working on a high mountain tree, as in this case, I leave the workshop door open so the wind blows in; I listen to powerful, dramatic music; and I recall the days I have spent in the Spanish Pyrenees, watching mountain goats as they skip along the ledges kicking rocks into the valley thousands of feet below. I guess this is what actors might call "getting into character." It might sound silly, but it works for me.

I had been considering the possibilities for some time, and by April 1998, I was ready to take the first steps. The lowest two branches were still sickly and had very little foliage left. There was a poorly executed shari just above them, which hadn't helped, but I think the main problem was that they were too remote for the naturally upward-growing tree to bother sustaining. Rather than cutting them off straight-away, I made them into long, sinuous jins. After all, they had interesting enough shapes that reflected the movement in the sharis higher up. I liked what I saw.

In fact, the more I considered the possibilities, the more I realized that all the older, curly branches were so full of dead wood they would be impossible to bend. The earlier pompons had extended, but there was no significant adventitious growth on the branches. Younger branches were, however, ripe for training. It began to dawn on me that by making jins of the more shapely branches, I would be able to preserve and even increase their visual impact, without having to wrestle with the problems of accommodating their far-flung foliage in a more compact design. So, off came their bark! I also extended a shari or two at the same time. In less than an hour, this rather placid, cotton-candy image had become full of drama and passion. Another two years passed before I began to tackle the foliage placement during a night of frenzied creativity.

I'd been itching to work on this juniper for ages. Then, one night in June 2000, it just hap-

March 1998. By now the lowest branches were so weak, they were clearly going to die. I took the plunge and made jins with them. I suddenly realized that by jinning other established branches, I could completely alter the dynamic of the material. It became more exciting, less sedate— much more to my taste.

pened. I always ponder my bonsai last thing at night. It's a wonderfully therapeutic way to unwind after a difficult day (or any other kind!). Sometimes, however, the pondering transmutes to fiddling—trying a few branches one way or another. Then, ominously, out comes the wire. "Just this one main branch—see how it looks..." Fatal! All recollections of my morning commitments dissolved, I was in that other place where bonsai nuts go when they're totally absorbed in their work. By the time I made it to bed, the sun was slanting through the window, casting on the wall dancing shadows of the birch tree outside; the birds had all but finished the finale of their dawn chorus, and the clatter of the 5:08 to Waterloo was fading into the distance. I was

April 1998. In order to get the plant to fit the unsuitable temporary pot, I had to compromise on the inclination. This was a mistake, and I should have known better. Always seek out a pot to suit the tree rather than shaping the tree to suit the nearest convenient pot.

larger, or at least different. I also wanted to formalize the foliage arrangement—far more so than the floppy arrangement in the original photograph, but not as contrived and incongruous as it appeared in 1994. The idea I had in mind was for the green area to be reasonably stable (albeit with its own integral movement) and for the jins and sharis to swirl through it in an apparently wild and uncontrolled manner.

The first step was to lower the apex. To achieve this, I had to split the live wood away from the dead for a short distance, at a point about halfway up the rising trunk. This wasn't the first time this had been done on this tree—many of the jins showed evidence of similar operations having taken place some time in the past. Even with 5mm copper wire, the trunk was reluctant to stay put, so I resorted to a tourniquet. Not the quickest way to persuade a branch to set in position but, in this case, the only one!

Next, I raised the lowest branch and brought it in toward the pot a little. Now I could begin the arrangement of the finer branches.

Although I wanted to compact and integrate the foliage areas, I certainly didn't want to create a single, solid green mass. It's essential to retain some distinction between the individual branch masses as well as between smaller elements within each branch mass. This need not be too pronounced—a mere visual hint will suffice. But without distinguishing between branch

happy. I hadn't finished the job by any means, but I knew by what I had done that it was going to work.

So, suitably armed with the appropriate attitude, I began wiring and shaping. I wanted to compact the foliage mass as much as possible without losing the cascading line. Compacting the foliage mass would allow the crazy jins to protrude, indicating that the tree had once been

By Spring 1999 I was becoming impatient. I wanted to secure the tree at the best angle before attempting any styling. I risked repotting again—just one year after the last session. Fortunately, I was able to change the pot and inclination with very little root disturbance.

These days I always use humate-based transplanting shock-reducing treatments whenever I feel I'm pushing a plant a little too far. I have conducted no scientific research, but I've read the reports from those who have, and the results seem impressive. Anyhow, it can't do any harm, and you never know....

Although the new pot was an undignified plastic affair, at least the planting angle was finally correct. I could now seriously consider the final design. The trunk had something to offer from several angles, which fitted nicely into my plan to create an all-round bonsai.

During my night of frenzied passion with this tree, I first cleaned all the old foliage from the branches (see page 66). This process not only prepares the tree to receive the wire, but it also prepares the artist to apply it.

You become more intimate with the tree and get to know all its peculiarities, such as the weak branch at the rear (above) that would never develop sufficiently to play a role in the design. Oh well, another jin....

Once you've decided on the best angle, how do you remember it when you transplant the tree? Simple—fashion a miniature plumb line and suspend it from a high point on the tree, so it hangs directly over another point. Mark both the top and bottom points with a waterproof marker.

masses the tree will not have that air of size, of majesty, that makes the bonsai image so much more powerful, so much more treelike. If you get the proportions and spacing just right, the image seems to buzz with electricity—not unlike what you might experience near high-tension power cables. It makes the hair on the back of your neck stand up and, for a brief moment, you have the feeling that you're somewhere else.

I needed four more long evening sessions to complete the restyling exercise. True, I could have done the job in one, but I can think of no reason why I should have. However, I can think of several why I should not.

First, much of the time is spent in what design types call visualizing (daydreaming would be nearer the truth...), getting the desired image and how it can be achieved firmly fixed in your mind. Working it out as you go is not the way to do it. When you know in advance which branches are going where, and why, you can plan your wiring more effectively. You can foresee potential problems later in the operation and avoid them; and you won't overstress the branches by repeated changes of mind. But, most importantly, you can focus more on the visual refinements.

Another good reason for taking your time is that you do a better job. Preparation, raffia, wiring, pruning, and placement are all done to a higher standard and this will be reflected in the outcome. As soon as the work becomes slightly

tedious, sit back and visualize some more—which brings me to the final reason for not rushing: I actually do this for pleasure. The entire process is immensely enjoyable, so I make it last.

Design analysis

In addition to my desire to create an all-round bonsai—one which could be viewed from all sides—I also wanted to create visual harmony among the trunks, the jins and the foliage masses. This was something that none of the previous owners seemed to have achieved. Somehow I had to bring order and stability to what was intrinsically chaotic.

The more exaggerated curves I introduced to the branches (particularly the lowest) and the rising trunk line now echo the lines of the jins, making it look more as if this is the natural growth habit of the tree in its particular environment. You can imagine how the jins were formed when you see living branches taking on a similar configuration. The design makes sense.

The rhythmic movement of the trunks is also echoed in the outlines of the major foliage masses. Here, again, harmonizing these elements has the effect of unifying and stabilizing the image. Neater and more clearly defined foliage masses lead to an illusion of a much bigger tree. Taking this one step further, by breaking up the large foliage masses into smaller

THE IMPORTANCE OF RAFFIA

When binding with raffia, take several strands together and soak them for ten minutes to soften them. Start by tying them around a convenient anchorage point, then bind tightly, overlapping by about half at each turn.

Before wiring heavy juniper branches I always bind them tightly with dyed raffia that has been soaked in water for a few minutes.

Why dyed raffia? Because I find the natural color of raffia offends the eye when working on the design—it is too visually prominent, like a freshly bleached jin, and can make assessing the visual balance unnecessarily difficult. This is especially true when the cream-colored raffia is crossed by 5mm brown wire!

Why soaked? Wet raffia has greater tensile strength than dry raffia, so it is less likely to snap as you pull it tight. (The idea that raffia shrinks as it dries is a myth—it doesn't!) Wet raffia is also easier to handle and control.

ones. The tree appears even bigger. The occasional glimpse of trunk or branch through the foliage adds life and credibility to the design.

There is still some development and refinement to be done—there always will be. For example, the lowest and middle branches need to be widened slightly because, from some angles, a little more integration of individual masses is needed. But I shall always maintain this light and airy image. Anything denser wouldn't look at all like a mountain cascade, but rather like a piece of topiary on someone's front porch.

What about the pot?

I'm in no rush to repot. I'd like to let the tree settle and regain vigor before disturbing the roots again. Besides, I'll have to wait three or four years for the image to mature, so there really is no rush. Repotting now would, in fact, slow the growth and I'd have to wait longer. In the meantime, I can think more carefully about the choice of pot.

I've already ruled out a crescent pot because the jins are where I want the random movement to be focused. If the jins were heavier, they might be able to compete with a crescent pot, but thin jins like these would be overpowered. Currently I fancy a fairly tall, parallel-sided pot, square in cross-section, with a dark, rocklike surface. But this is likely to change many times before I finally decide.

Although the copper wire was strong enough to introduce gentle lateral movement, it was nowhere near strong enough to bend the trunk down. In cases like this you have to resort to a tourniquet. Notice how unobtrusive the colored raffia is.

In order to lower the apex, I had to separate the living tissue from the dead wood to enable that section to bend. I started the split with a saw cut and extended it with brute force.

Why use raffia at all? Well, you can use plastic tape or any number of substitutes, but raffia seems always to be the best choice. It's organic (the leaf bast of the raphia palm) so it "breathes." It disintegrates after about a year, so it doesn't constrict the vascular system of the branch. And when properly applied, it has a considerable cushioning effect between wire and bark.

When binding a branch with raffia, take half a dozen flat strands together and bind them tightly around the branch. Overlap them at each turn to build up thickness for cushioning and to ensure that there are no weak areas. Make sure that both ends are securely tied.

I applied raffia to some of the thinner branches on this tree. The branches were quite old and had been shaped and pruned several times—not always very well, resulting in many minor sharis and inclusions of dead wood. Chinese juniper snaps easily at these points, and I didn't want to take chances!

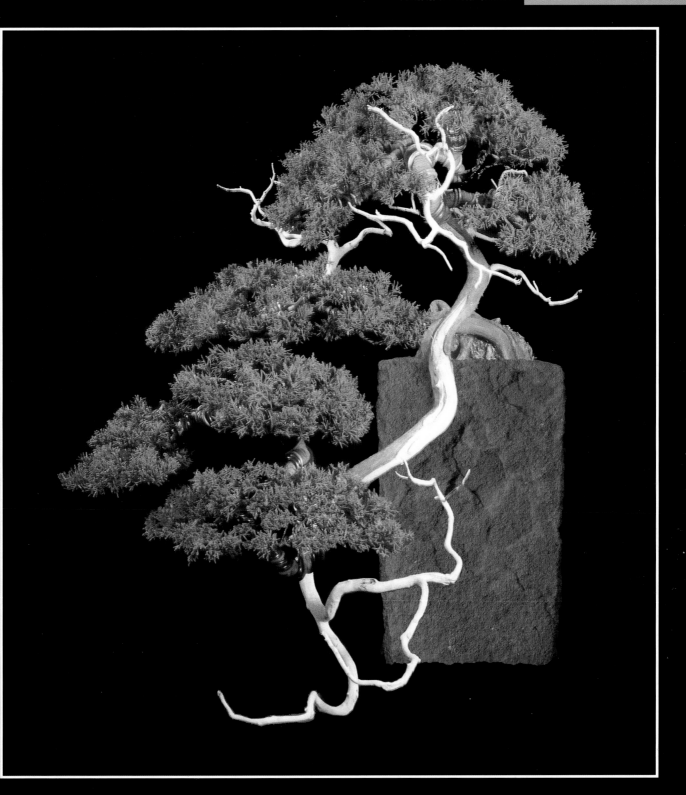

Shimpaku juniper

Summer 2000

**6.5 inches (18cm) high;
5.5 inches (14cm) wide.**

*The wind may blow through a
forest in one direction, but the branches
swirl and dance this way and that.*

Pines

THE SHEER MAJESTY of full-grown pines has few comparisons, and the Scots pine (named after Sir Walter Scot) is surely the king of them all. Its size—up to 100 ft (over 30m) or more in Scotland—and its blue-tinted foliage make an imposing sight against the clear blue sky. It's amazing how such a gigantic tree, with needles up to four inches (10cm) long can be perfectly happy living in a tiny container with needles reduced to less than a quarter of that size.

In spite of their sulking reaction to being hoisted from open ground, once established in a pot, Scots pines are as tough and forgiving as any species. They tolerate near-drought conditions for extended periods and are just as accommodating when asked to live in the wettest of climates.

Above all, the one aspect of pines that I find the most enchanting is the regular pattern formed by neatly wired and precisely positioned shoots. Each tuft of needles occupies its own space, pointing skyward—like a multitude of people with arms raised to greet the sun.

New pine shoots in late spring. Those in front are from a pine in training, while those at the rear are from a full-size tree.

More a bonsai than a tree

SHOHIN SCOTS PINE

Pinus sylvestris (Scots pine)

The outstanding Japanese-American bonsai artist, John Yoshio Naka, once advised: "Don't try to make your tree look like a bonsai, make your bonsai look like a tree." We would all be well advised to take this message to heart.

MUCH HAS been written about developing raw material and its subsequent styling, but those are merely the very early stages in the life of a bonsai. Once the basic style and branch placement has been established, there follows a period of consolidation—ramification increases, the foliage becomes denser, and the leaves and needles reduce in size.

In due course, however, a bonsai reaches a stage that you regard as its peak. You're content with the image you've created. For a few years you maintain its form and character by careful pinching and pruning, but before long, you begin to realize that the tree has passed its peak—it somehow doesn't look quite so "right." The outer shoots will almost invariably have become congested and the canopy will have expanded little by little. The trunk may have thickened, influencing the character of the tree: from graceful or elegant to powerful and masculine. As branches thicken and ramify or become gnarled with constant hard pruning, they increase in visual power as well as physical bulk. This may make some branches redundant or even undesirable—if not immediately, then certainly in the foreseeable future.

When a bonsai arrives at this stage, the artist is faced with several options. One option is to remodel the tree entirely; another is to develop the tree into a larger bonsai; a third is to reinstate the bonsai's former aesthetic peak. Whatever the decision, the artist must always be thinking several years ahead, just as when imposing the original design.

This is inevitable with all bonsai, regardless of species or size, no matter how skillfully it has been maintained. Only the timescale changes because that depends very much on species and size: small trees or coarse, vigorous species will need more frequent remodeling or renovation than larger trees. Here we will look at the timescale of the development of a shohin Scots pine (*Pinus sylvestris*) and the attempt to improve on its current structure while honoring the original design concept.

This little pine started its bonsai life in 1983 as a three year-old seedling. It was one of many thousands that were growing in a tract of open heath and had been trampled by wild horses or deer. This particular seedling had produced half a dozen adventitious shoots growing from the cotyledon node on the stem, which was quite severely bent. I cut off everything apart from three of these shoots and allowed them to grow freely for three years before doing any pinching or pruning. Thereafter, until 1992, I pinched back all the candles (extending shoots) to half their length each spring.

In 1990, I cut off two of the original three branches, leaving only the central one to form the upper trunk. This was really the first time that I had seriously considered the bonsai's final size and design. The two branches that I removed were almost directly opposite each other. Although the one on the right was higher on the trunk, the trunk angle made it seem lower than it really was. I converted this branch to a jin and cut the other off completely because opposing or bar jins are equally as jarring to the eye as opposing branches. The resulting wound was really rather ugly at this stage, but experience told me that this scar would eventually heal and become almost imperceptible. It wasn't until spring 1992 that I decided on the initial branch placement and began training in earnest.

Design Considerations

All pines will bud back on older wood given sufficiently high nitrogen in the fertilizer and regular pinching and pruning, although some are less eager than others. Fortunately, Scots pine is one of the most obliging in this regard, which makes it an ideal species for shohin as well as for larger bonsai. However, given the inevitable disproportion between the size of the bonsai and the length of the needles—minimum of three-quarters of an inch (18mm)—the open, treelike styles that are normally employed for Scots pine are impossible to achieve on a shohin unless one settles for a neo-literati. Instead, one must resort to a more abstract bonsai style.

The emergence of a less treelike bonsai style has only really taken place during the last two decades. During this period, the preferred ratio of trunk thickness to height reduced from around 1:6 or 1:8 down to 1:4 or even 1:3. In practice, this means that various training and styling techniques (not all of them good, by any means) were devised in order to achieve the new look. One such development is what one might call the "cupola" style, variously referred to by those who disapprove of it as the "tin-helmet" or "umbrella" style.

I personally regard this style as less merit-worthy than more naturalistic forms, and have even described it in disparaging terms from time to time—but only when it has been done for the sake of following fashion. Too often wonderful collected pines and junipers, with

You have to start somewhere.... This rather scruffy little seedling was selected because it appeared to have denser growth than is normal for Scots pines. At this stage I had no idea what I was going to do with it, but I knew it had the characteristics I was looking for.

the potential to be trained into exciting, majestic and awe-inspiring images of trees, have been forced into compact, dense domes which might well, for the time being, look like good bonsai but will never actually be good bonsai trees.

So, because of the diminutive size of this plant, I decided on the tin-helmet style. The trunk was—and still is—too narrow for the overall bulk of the tree, but it will thicken in time as they always do. Also, as the cycles of growth and reduction, and shaping and reshaping continues, new buds will form further back along the branches. I will gradually reduce the overall width of the tree by pruning back to these new buds in stages. Hopefully, before I shuffle off this mortal coil, the trunk and foliage mass will have achieved more pleasing proportions.

After the initial branch placement, the tree

REGIONAL STYLES?

In recent years I've become aware of regional differences in preferred bonsai styles. In southern Europe, almost all conifers and many broad-leaved species are forced into low, compact domes. In northern Europe bonsai growers seem to prefer taller, fuller images.

Some of this difference could be attributed to the greater influence of Japanese teaching in southern Europe, but I believe there is a more deep-rooted cause.

In northern Europe, a 200-year-old pine or oak may be 80 feet (25m) tall. In the south, the same tree would only grow to around 30 feet (10m). The same thing happens at high altitude. To people from northern Europe an old tree is lofty with heavy arching branches. To those from the south—or from mountainous regions—an old tree is low, dense and spreading with a heavy trunk.

You don't need to think about creating regional styles—it happens all on its own!

The initial work involved merely shaping and positioning the main branches. At this stage there is no need to worry about all the smaller shoots—they should be left to strengthen and develop adventitious buds before shaping.

One of the so-called rules of bonsai design states that the lowest branch should be located approximately at one third of the height of the trunk. This is a classic example of a rule that should be interpreted rather than followed. It matters little where the first branch originates. The critical factor is the position of the lowest tier of foliage, which may be supported by a steeply cascading branch (as here) or even on a subsidiary trunk.

was still little more than a jumble of branches and needles, although I could clearly see the interesting trunk line and the rationale behind the positioning of the branches. Wiring high branches way down below horizontal is a useful technique. It enables you to create a fuller image with several tiers of foliage without the need to grow a taller tree. It's not entirely unnatural either, which satisfies my personal requirement for credibility in bonsai design.

During the original training session, I didn't wire any of the smaller branchlets. There was no point in doing so. I had the final image I wanted to create firmly in mind and knew I would need lots more back-budding and increased ramification to achieve it. Wiring the smaller branchlets would have decreased their vigor and retarded the overall development of the tree. This in turn would have extended the time needed for the major branches to set in position. Wiring a tree in stages like this may seem a rather prolonged and overcautious approach. But, in cases when more growth is needed to complete the design, it actually leads to an established image a season or two sooner than the "wire everything at once" strategy. If you are dealing with a very well prepared, densely ramified piece of raw material, then sure, wire everything in sight. But with my little pine, that was not the case.

For the next three years I fed cleverly and

viciously pinched back the candles in summer to encourage the back-budding and consequent ramification I wanted. In order to allow the tiny new buds on older wood room to develop, I also kept the branches free of old needles at all times, cutting them rather than pulling them out. Normally, on an established pine, I would pull out the old needles in the fall, but on a developing tree, especially a small one, I prefer to cut them in mid- to late summer.

Eliminating needles during the same growth phase as pinching the extending candles creates the maximum possible disturbance at a time when the tree is growing at its maximum rate. It's hardly surprising that this induces the maximum amount of back-budding. Cutting, rather than pulling, eliminates the risk of yanking out embryonic buds concealed in the sheath at the base of the needles. The inevitable and rather unsightly browning and eventual shedding of the remains of the needles doesn't matter on a developing tree as much as on an established specimen.

I finally wired the smaller branches and established the complete framework in late summer 1995. There was sufficient space between the tiers of foliage to define them in the future if the length of the needles could be reduced, which is not difficult. The next stage in development was to induce new buds in the inner areas of the branch framework to fill in the voids and to build a little height to the tiers.

By fall 1997 I was more or less satisfied with the overall image. The general shape of the canopy and the inter-branch spaces worked well together, balancing nicely with the movement in the trunk. I was still a little disappointed at the lack of sufficient increase in girth of the trunk, but in time...! To give an idea of scale, the pot measures 9" (240mm) wide, and the tree is 12" (300mm) tall.

At this point I was happy enough with the tree to exhibit it, braving the taunts of my peers who were painfully aware of my dislike for the tin-helmet style. I naturally argued that the inter-branch spaces disqualified the tree from that style but, alas, my protests were in vain. Fortunately my critics were so enthusiastic in their efforts to make me blush, none seemed to notice the rather poor nebari! The surface roots have always been too thick and brittle to bend significantly, but at each repotting they are moved a little. This and my eternal helper—

FEEDING FOR A PURPOSE

Scots pines are gratifyingly predictable in their response to feeding and pinching strategies. The nature and timing of both will influence the number and, to a large extent, the location of adventitious buds.

Scots pines are genetically programmed to produce just one flush of growth each year, although on occasion abnormal conditions might induce a weak second flush. We can create these abnormal conditions by pinching the candles or pruning in early summer. But we can also use the tree's one-flush cycle to our advantage as well.

Assuming that the pine in question has reached a satisfactory size and girth, and has already received its initial training, the normal feeding pattern should be reversed. When you think about it, it's really quite logical. Our aim is to achieve three goals:

- Tight ramification with short internodes
- Short, compact needles
- Prolific adventitious buds on older wood

So, in spring, feed sparingly with a low-nitrogen or nitrogen-free fertilizer. This will keep the vigor of the extending candles to a minimum. The needles will be shorter and so will the distances between each pair of needles. Therefore, any adventitious buds that might emerge on that section of the branch in the future will be closer together—in other words, shorter internodes.

As the candles lose their papery sheath and the needles prepare to peel away from the shoot, use a more balanced feed, but make sure that the nitrogen content is still no greater than either the potassium or phosphorus. Do this about a week or two before pinching begins. This will ensure that the vigor has increased by the time you pinch the extending candles, so new buds will form readily at the point of severance. If the tree is particularly vigorous, continue with low-nitrogen until pinching has begun.

As soon as the needles have pulled away from the shoot by about 45°, provided the watering is carefully controlled *(see page 110)* they won't grow any longer, so you can increase the nitrogen content once more. The tree will be urged to produce more vegetative growth, but it can't because it is programmed not to. Besides, you have very sneakily robbed it of all its primary buds! However, all this nitrogen-induced growth energy has to go somewhere, so the tree will pump it all into producing plenty of healthy, adventitious buds in readiness for next spring. The higher the nitrogen content in this phase, the more prolific and vigorous the back-budding. If there are any of the previous winter's adventitious buds that haven't opened, they may do so now, but they will only form small rosettes of needles. Look after these delicate small shoots by allowing them light and air and by a little judicious pruning of outer growth on the same branch if appropriate.

If, as a result of this hyper-feeding a late second flush of growth results, regard this as a bonus.

Steady feeding with low nitrogen in spring and high nitrogen in late summer, combined with pinching off about three-quarters of each candle just as the needles begin to peel away from the shoot, induces the back-budding necessary to the development and maintenance of all pines. These tiny buds are on branches that are at least fifteen years old (apologies for the wire scar—it happens to all of us!). Buds usually develop visibly in late summer.

The following year, after the candles have been pinched, the new buds break but generally don't extend into proper candles. Instead they form rosettes of needles. Once they reach this stage it is safe to prune back to them and await their further development the following year. Pruning back to a bud that hasn't yet broken will almost invariably lead to that bud aborting and the death of the remaining branch as far back as the next foliage-bearing shoot.

ABOVE: Fall 1997. By now my little pine had reached its optimum stage—the branch lines were still visible but the foliage was dense and compact.

When viewed from the side, the uniformity of branch distribution around the trunk is evident. Moreover, you can clearly see that the trunk curves toward the front.

This pine is so vigorous, it regularly sets up to eight buds at around the tip of pinched candles. These need to be thinned to only two buds.

time—will gradually bring about the necessary improvements.

Trees grow each year. That's the way nature is, and it is our task to control this growth so the total bulk of the foliage appears not to increase. On a medium or large bonsai an annual increase in bulk of a quarter to a half an inch (6 – 12mm) is of little consequence and can easily be reduced without the need for major restructuring. But on a small bonsai, such an increase can easily destroy the proportions of the design, and any temporary remedial pruning will probably exacerbate the problem for the following year. Such pruning—in fact all pruning—should be done bearing in mind the future development, not the present image.

One year after exhibiting this bonsai at what I considered to be its peak, I found it to be overgrown. By fall 1998, the foliage bulk had clearly outgrown the design. I had pinched all the candles back extremely hard, leaving only four or five pairs of needles on each. Nevertheless, they were sufficient in number to have a significant effect on the image, even though the average needle length was only around one inch (25mm). In addition, the total number of shoots had almost doubled since the previous year, so the visual weight of the canopy had increased substantially and most of the inter-branch spaces had all but filled in.

These inter-branch spaces are essential to bonsai design and never more so than on small pines. Without them you have, at best, a bush (read "tin helmet") or something that resembles a table lamp, with them you have a tree. Clearly the time had come to progress this pine to the next stage.

When looking at a full-size tree, to have the whole tree in your field of vision, you need to stand a considerable distance away from it. Therefore the difference between the distance from your eye to the base of the tree and the distance from your eye to the apex is negligible. However, when you have a bonsai filling your field of vision, you are standing much closer, so this ratio increases. You don't notice it consciously (unless you're looking for it) but your brain registers this fact and tells you that you're looking at a miniature tree close up. Inclining the apex toward the front decreases the distance from your eye to that part of the tree, thus creating the illusion that you're looking at a much bigger tree from further away.

Late summer 1998: The increase in bulk since the previous year (see opposite) is alarming. The branch lines are totally hidden and the mass of the canopy makes the trunk seem ridiculously spindly. Clearly something must be done.

BELOW: Before taking this picture, I had already plucked most of the old needles and pruned away some long, straggly shoots that had been used to fill vacant areas in the periphery of some of the foliage masses. Now the unruly structure is more obvious.

Stage 2: structural refinement

I decided to try to improve the outer branch formation in such a way that, next time the tree reached its peak, it might remain there for rather more than just one year. Some secondary branches could easily be removed to help pre-serve inter-branch spaces. Many of the young outer shoots could now also be removed, using new growth from the back-budding to replace the peripheral shoots.

The trick is to position each shoot so that the one or two buds at its tip have room to extend a fraction and double in number during the next few growing seasons. It's also necessary to antic-ipate the growth of any adventitious buds and leave room for them to develop. Looking even further into the future, the new shoots that grow from the adventitious buds will eventually replace some of the existing framework, so this, too, must be considered. When restructuring any bonsai you need to create and memorize a sort of mental blueprint for the tree's develop-ment and stick to it from year to year.

PRINCIPLES OF CANDLE-PINCHING

When feeding, pinching and pruning are all calculated properly, viable adventitious buds will form on wood that is many years old—certainly old enough to have mature, flaky bark. This amazing proliferation of buds was achieved on a Scots pine that was collected from the wild only two years previously!

If a pine shoot, or candle, is severed while it is still young and extending, it will respond by producing buds at the point of severance—up to four or five, depending on the vigor, size and age of the tree. If a shoot is severed when it is one year old but still bearing needles, it will produce buds between the pairs of needles at various points on its length, not usually at the tip. If the shoot is severed halfway between these two times, guess what? ...It produces buds at the tip as well as further back!

Naturally, there are many other factors that influence the number and viability of these buds, such as feeding, climate, vigor, and so on. But the principle is constant and the timing can be adjusted to achieve the desired reaction.

Another influential factor that we use is the severity of pinching. Generally speaking, the more you remove, the more buds will form. A tree's growing buds (candles in the case of pines) pruduce hormones (auxins) that inhibit the growth of buds further back along the branch. The more of the candles you remove, the greater will be the reduction in the growth-inhibiting auxins, so the more latent buds are stimulated to grow.

When you're developing your Scots pine, you need strong, prolific buds on old wood to use for the branch framework. Allow the new candles to extend fully and the needles to peel away a little, then cut them right back to the base. A cluster of buds will form at this point during fall and winter. These buds will be fat and strong and will produce vigorous new candles the following year. More buds will form on older wood, especially where some old needles remain. These will be prolific and small at first, so keep careful watch. Don't attempt to pull out the needles on either side of a bud or you will bring the bud away with them. The next year, pinching the terminal shoots earlier will spur the smaller back buds into growth.

An amazing 73 shoots were pruned away, many of them several years old and bearing secondary shoots.

The best time of year to carry out this restructuring work is early fall or early spring. I favor early fall because the adventitious buds will strengthen over winter in response to the pruning and partial defoliation. Also, spring is usually too short to complete all the tasks that have to be done at that time. Anything that can be done in the fall, should be.

First I pulled out all the previous season's needles as well as some of the current year's, leaving a cluster at the tip of each shoot—like a rosette of cedar needles. This is an important practice for three reasons: it enables you to examine and assess the branch structure more easily; it enables wire to be applied efficiently; it further encourages the production of even more adventitious buds on older wood.

When you start building the tertiary branches and developing ramification, pinch the candles earlier, when they are semimature and the needles are clearly discernible but still hug the shoot. Pinch them to a precise length—that which you want before the next fork in the branch. You know you will get at least one bud at the broken tip, probably several. If you do only get one, you know that cutting back that hard the following year will give you more. If only we could develop other species so precisely....

Once the pine has become established and you merely want to maintain the balanced image for as long as possible, you should pinch the candles very early, when the needles are still shrouded in papery filaments. You must leave sufficient needles to nourish the tree and keep it healthy, but no more. Pinch off about two-thirds to three-quarters. Some buds will still form on older wood from time to time, which you want anyway, but they will be fairly small and not so numerous.

Whenever you pinch candles, always start with the weakest part of the tree, usually on the lower branches, and finish with the stronger areas a week or two later. This ensures that the weaker areas begin to regenerate new buds before the strongest areas steal all the energy.

Next, I shortened or removed over seventy shoots, mostly around the periphery, but also some closer to the trunk. Some of these shoots were little more than rosettes, but many were several years old and supported their own secondary shoots. I also cut off one branch on the left-hand side. The branches had developed and gained bulk over the preceding years and there was now no need for so many. Removing the one branch and gently repositioning the others enabled me to allow more inter-branch spacing while still retaining the same overall form. A classic example of the "less is more" maxim.

Once I had reduced the bulk of vegetation sufficiently, I wired every branch and every shoot, carefully positioning them according to my mental blueprint.

Renovation completed. One branch—emerging close to the trunk on the second left-hand branch—has been eliminated, leaving a jin. This allows a clearer view of the trunk line. All branches have been pulled downward in varying degrees, so they all display a similar sweeping movement. This is a great improvement in the harmony of the design. Pulling the branches down this way also creates more space between them, and that will make the maintenance of the optimum image much less of a chore.

Whatever the age, style or maturity of the tree in front of him, the bonsai artist must always think several years ahead, just as when imposing the original design.

This bird's-eye view of the lower left branch shows the arangement of the secondary branches and the shoots. I worked on the principle of using the smallest number of shoots to fill the maximum area. Vacant spaces that were filled with visible buds were filled with shoots wired into position from nearby. Shoots for which no place could be found were ruthlessly eliminated. You can see how almost all the remaining shoots have developed from adventitious buds.

A bird's-eye view of the apex (front at the top of the picture). Note that there is no central leader. A mature apex should be formed in the same way as a branch—but with two differences. First, the secondary branches radiate in all directions. Second, it is supported from beneath rather than from one side. The belief that the apex should be modeled like a miniature tree is erroneous. If that were true, the apex would have yet another miniature tree on top of it... ad infinitum.

Fall 1999: a year after restructuring. The image is still a little light, which means it is likely to achieve its ideal form in 2000 and remain in that state for some time. Compare this picture with the one taken in 1992 (page 94)—you can see how the original plan came to fruition.

When a tree has just undergone a major restructuring like this, it shouldn't look perfect. It should look as if it has just received a military haircut. (Okay, some may regard that as perfect, but not I.) If the tree looks perfect at this stage, the next year it will have already outgrown its design yet again. I repeat: the purpose of these restructuring sessions is to create a framework of branches and buds that will allow the tree the maximum period of perfect or near perfect appearance before the next remodeling session becomes due.

Although the trunk had at last thickened somewhat during the year since 1997 (inevitable, considering the bulk of the foliage during that time), it now appeared to be even thicker still, because of the reduced visual weight of the tree as a whole. The pruning and wiring seemed to have had a dramatic, invigorating effect, because during 1999 the trunk thickened more than in any other year.

Throughout the remodeling process, 73 shoots were pruned away, mainly from the peripheral area. Some were little more than buds with a rosette of needles surrounding them, but many were several years old and had ramified. One secondary branch was also removed in addition to the shoots.

Scots pine—shohin

Summer 2000

**10 inches (26cm) high; 10 inches (26cm) wide.
Japanese pot**

An improbable pine

FLACCID TRUNKS AND OTHER DISORDERS
Pinus sylvestris (Scots pine)

If you have an eye for the bizarre—or can develop one— you can break through the barriers of traditional bonsai design and create truly unique images that are more evocative of majestic wild trees than of the tedious repetition of classical bonsai.

TREES IN THE wild don't conform to any arbitrary set of stylistic rules. They're governed by a combination of their own genetic program and the environmental conditions in which they live. The wilder these conditions, the more the tree's natural habit has to adapt. For instance, a lowland pine in a temperate climate will have a sturdy, straight trunk bearing a uniform cone of branches almost to ground level when young. When mature, its crown becomes broad and rounded; some of the lower branches will fail, but many will remain and become heavy, pendulous boughs, maintaining a full, rich image. Here, the tree's natural habit prevails.

On the other hand, a lone pine growing in the wilderness will adopt an entirely different appearance. The harsh environment and poor soil will override the tree's genetic program. Branches are shed early; growth changes direction dramatically as terminal shoots are bitten off by freezing winds or withered by drought.

A pine growing high in the mountains will quickly become compressed by heavy snows and intense, unfiltered sunlight, forming a low, spreading dome of tangled branches. These images form the basis of the neoclassical driftwood styles that are so popular today—bridging the gap between classical design and free-form sculpture.

A pine growing in the rocky peat soil of the exposed Scottish highlands, where the growing season is short, will be drawn skyward as the longer low branches are whipped by the wind until they snap. The race to replace the lost foliage conspires with the constant directional changes of terminal growth to produce slender, angular trunks whose chaotic lines dance beneath an understated, delicately poised canopy—*bunjin* style in nature.

In the inhospitable peat bogs that form a part of the New Forest in southern England, Scots pines are the only trees that can survive. Their incredible tenacity enables them to counter constant saturation of the roots, regular winter freezing and an almost nutrient-free diet. But here they never achieve maturity. By the time they have grown as tall as a man they are already in serious decline. They flower, they set seed and soon they die, littering the barren landscape with their skeletal remains, bleached silver by the sun and wind.

In such places, the groundcover consists mainly of rank grasses and rushes that can grow waist-high. No browsing animals are prepared to brave the swamp—they have no need to, because there is ample food on drier land. Seedlings germinate only rarely, and when they do, they scramble their way through the surrounding rushes to find sunlight and fresh air. Many are stifled before the end of the first season but some, just a few, make it through and live long enough for the slow cycle of regeneration to continue.

I only collect wild trees very rarely. When I see these stubborn plants in their natural habitat I am filled with admiration and I'm loath to rob others of the opportunity to enjoy them in the future. Occasionally self-indulgence wins out and I do collect trees, but only from areas where they are in reasonable abundance, and only one from any single location.

THE RANGE OF SCOTS PINES

The range of climates and conditions tolerated by Scots pines is enormous. They thrive in the bitter cold winters and short summers north of the Arctic Circle. They are equally happy in the intense heat of Spain, provided they can find some brief respite in winter. They will live for many months in rocky soil without a drop of rain but will also survive to maturity in wetlands and marshes. Traditionally, pines prefer acidic soils, yet the mighty Scots pine grows in abundance on limestone and even the chalk downs of southern England.

A classically beautiful Scots pine growing in the London suburbs. The tree was there long before the houses were built.

On one of my rare collecting trips to the New Forest I came across a small pine that my two companions rejected because of its diminutive proportions. I wouldn't have even noticed it myself had I not sat on a tussock of grass in order to take off my boots and pour out the cold, stagnant water that had leaked into them. Right next to me, peeping through the winter-brown grass were three small tufts of pine foliage. It becomes second nature for a bonsai addict to investigate any nearby woody plant, so I idly traced the trunk of one of these tufts down through the soggy grass. Much to my surprise, I discovered that all three tufts were part of the same plant, and that the three stems ("trunk" is too dignified a word to describe them) all met at ground level. This is very rare with pines—especially with Scots pines—because they never sprout from old wood or from below the cotyledon node. This pine must have been nipped in the bud immediately after germination and miraculously survived the ordeal.

The tree was clearly very weak—so weak that any root disturbance might well prove fatal. Besides, it was a cold February afternoon and the light was fading fast. I was wet, miserable and hungry, and my feet were becoming numb. There was only one way I was going to get this tree home and that was to take the entire tussock and worry about the next stage in the relative comfort of my workshop. So, after three or four swift swipes of the spade I was able to lift 40 pounds of forest floor onto my shoulder and trudge off toward the road. I'm not sure what made my companions laugh the most—the fact that I appeared to have collected nothing more than a giant load of sod, or the sight of me suddenly sinking to my chest in the bog as I misjudged my step. Having exhausted my extensive vocabulary of expletives, the ridiculousness of the situation dawned on me also. Hysterical laughter does not make the task of scrambling out of a bog easy, especially with a now even wetter and heavier load. Since I was already soaked to the skin and couldn't get any wetter, I completed the journey by wading through the channels with images of Humphrey Bogart in *African Queen* in mind (minus the leeches, thank heaven!).

Unearthing the challenge

I have to admit that the discomfort and effort involved in collecting this little tree seemed at first to be far more than its apparent potential justified. Nevertheless, there it was, and once I'd dried off and warmed my innards with a cup of hot beef broth I set to work trimming back the grass and rushes. Whenever possible I prefer to bare-root all newly collected trees before potting, but sometimes the roots of the tree are so entangled with other roots that this would be too risky. I suspected that this might be the case here but as soon as I began to tug at the outer clumps of grass the entire root ball fell apart. Lucky me! The tree itself had three main roots and a surprising amount of fine roots. It appeared to have been living in the humus-rich soil of the tussock and had not allowed its roots to extend any further. After soaking the roots in a humate-based transplanting solution for thirty

I'll resist the temptation here to preach too much about the immorality of over-collecting to satisfy greed or ego; this is a matter for each of us to reconcile with our own conscience. Suffice it to say that bonsai is an art, not a sport. Our work is judged by the quality of what we do with out hands and minds, not by the quantity of potential bonsai we can accumulate in as short a time as possible. One masterpiece is worth much, much more than a yard full of dead and dying failures—and the joy of appreciating that one bonsai year after year far exceeds the ephemeral thrill of the initial hunt and capture of the prey.

The mature bark of a typical full-grown Scots pine in a temperate climate. The orange tint of the raised plates is never seen in stunted trees. On the upper trunk and on the heavy branches the bark is papery and bright orange.

This finer, more flaky mature bark texture appears on Scots pines that have been growing in poorly drained soil in regions with high rainfall.

When a Scots pine is grown vigorously in fertile garden soil and regularly clipped, it produces a heavy foliage burden but the trunk doesn't expand very rapidly. Under these circumstances, the bark can develop convincing fissures like these within four or five years.

BARK TEXTURE

Mature, textured bark is arguably the most precious feature of almost any bonsai. Most species develop perticular bark characteristics as they mature, usually adopting a fissured, or plated, texture.

New layers of bark are formed annually in much the same way the annual rings are formed. The single-cell thick cambium layer produces new xylem on the inside and new phloem on the outside. As each new layer of phloem is formed, the outermost layer dies and becomes bark.

Speed of growth is not the controlling factor. If a tree grows very rapidly, it can reach a considerable size and age without displaying mature bark. The dying phloem remains elastic, and the stretching process associated with rapid trunk expansion retards the development of bark texture.

The amount of phloem laid down each year in comparison with the trunk expansion is one factor that determines how quickly the bark will mature. The amount of phloem produced is, in turn, governed by the amount of foliage on the tree. A slowly expanding trunk with a heavy foliage burden will lay down a comparatively thick annual phloem deposit, and will, in turn, produce more bark, which will mature quicker.

Another factor that influences bark texture is the environment in which the tree is growing. Whether the trunk is kept constantly moist or exposed to hot sun; the fertility and acidity of the local soil; the availability of water to the roots; and the length of the growing season all seem to have some noticeable effect on the texture of the mature bark.

minutes, I was able to wash away all the remaining soil and plant the tree in a conveniently small container, using a very gritty soil mix.

Never have I seen a pine respond so well to transplanting. It was as if it had been set free—like a bird that has just learned to fly. During the next two years the vigor of the growth was phenomenal. I pinched back the extending candles in the normal way but the back-budding was far more prolific than I have ever experienced. By

the end of the second season in a container, my weird little pine was begging to be worked on.

The design challenge was twofold. First, the central trunk of the trio was much thinner than the others, and very long. This broke the so-called rules of bonsai design, which state that the thinnest trunk in any group should be shorter than the others and positioned at the rear of the composition. The other challenge was more bizarre. The central trunk was clearly

LEFT: *Even though it's only growing in a small container, the growth has been phenomenal during the two years since collection from the wild. Improved soil conditions, more light and a good feeding program have guaranteed the total rejuvenation of this previously fragile pine. It's certainly now strong enough to be worked on.*

BELOW: *The way the central trunk is sandwiched between the others makes it seem like an afterthought. It was clearly originally a weak shoot that somehow survived long enough to force its way through the grasses to find the light.*

Without the support of surrounding plants, the flaccid central trunk collapses onto its neighbor. Even though it has been growing vigorously for two years while being supported in a more vertical position, it seems to have gained no structural strength at all.

younger than the others—an afterthought of nature—and had been drawn up through the grasses to find light very quickly. It was so leggy it didn't have the strength to support its own weight. During the two years of establishment I had propped it up with a bamboo stick, hoping that it would gain strength. Fat chance! As soon as I removed the support, the spindly trunk fell flat on its side!

I discovered that this tree was becoming famous locally. My two collecting companions reveled in relating the story of how I struggled through the bog with a giant sod on my shoulder only to discover that I had collected a seemingly worthless piece of material. When they saw the flaccid central trunk, they just couldn't contain their mirth. Their (and everyone else's) immediate advice was to cut out the thin trunk and try to make something with the other two. Now, I love a challenge, and offering such advice is like a red rag to a bull. The more they tried to persuade me to do this, the more I dug my heels in. Besides, this pine was truly unique, and that was an important consideration for a rebel like me! I was determined to make this tree work somehow—but how?

The technique I used to strengthen the weak trunk was fairly straightforward if rather intricate. Bear in mind that the trunk was little more than pencil-thick.

I used a sharp scalpel to remove a strip of bark, thus ensuring a clean edge that would heal more efficiently.

The channel was routed using a minute bit in a Dremel power tool.

Coping with a flaccid pine

In order to add strength to the trunk, I decided to embed a wire in the trunk throughout its entire length—an adaptation of a fairly common technique used for accomplishing severe bends in juniper branches. I'll admit at the outset that, although I was confident that it would work eventually, I did make two mistakes at the first attempt. I learned a few lessons and would approach the problem differently in future.

The flimsy trunk was only three-eighths of an inch (10mm) thick, so I had to work very carefully. I used the little flat sawlike cutting wheel on my Dremel to cut a groove the entire length of the trunk, on what I anticipated would be the rear. I cut right through to the heart—over halfway through the trunk—wherever I could, or wherever I dared! I made this channel just a little too small to accommodate a strand of 2.5mm wire and cleaned the edges with a surgical scalpel afterwards. This brought the aperture to precisely the right size for the wire.

Mistake number one: I should have cut even deeper to bury the wire exactly in the center of the trunk. when the time came, I was unable to push the wire in quite that far. My nervousness prevented me from being bolder. Oh, well, faint heart never won fair bonsai....

I cut the wire to length and forced it into the

Adventitious buds like these, which are essential for maintaining the shape of an established pine, are strengthened and stimulated to extend by regular careful plucking of old needles.

After inserting the wire as far as it would go, I filed the channel with cut-paste and bound the trunk tightly with raffia.

Although the wire had clearly added considerable strength and rigidity to the trunk, during the next two years resin deposits forced the wire out of the channel, so the whole process had to be repeated and improved.

NEEDLE-PLUCKING SCOTS PINES

"Summer fades to mist
Old needles rain from the pines
Springs beneath my feet."

'Scuse the haiku, but it illustrates beautifully the natural shedding of pine needles in autumn. Older needles fade from green, through dull yellow, to brown before carpeting the ground below with a thick, springy layer. Look again at the last line of the haiku and read it out loud. It could just as easily be written, "Spring's beneath my feet," meaning spring is just around the corner; needle shedding is in preparation for the next season's growth. In spring more needles may fall as new candles extend. It's to do with economy of the tree's resources, just as it is with deciduous trees, but on a different schedule.

Bonsai are much denser than natural pines, and needles tend to remain longer because of the limited growth we permit. For both these reasons, the annual needle-plucking festival takes place in late summer or early autumn. Happy, smiling bonsai folks sit at their benches and pluck out all the previous year's needles one by one. Or they should! This tedious chore is often the one that gets missed, but it is an important one in the maintenance program. Happily, if you miss the autumn festival, you can join the spring needle-pluckers instead—no excuse!

It's important to work slowly, pulling only one needle at a time, so that the sheath at the base of each pair of needles remains intact wherever possible. The tiny latent buds that nestle between the needles are very fragile. If you pull away a pair of needles with the sheath, peel them apart carefully and you'll see the minute bud still stuck to one of them.

Once the needles have been plucked out, the buds are stimulated to expand. Not all buds do extend, but the tree will find a way to reach the right balance. Naturally, the healthier and more vigorous the tree, the more buds will develop *(see page 96)*.

Needle plucking also balances the vigor in different parts of the tree. Plucking fewer needles on the lower branches than at the apex will keep them strong.

Pulling needles from a semi-ripe candle often stimulates the rapid production of new buds to replace the missing needles. These characteristically open as rosettes of flattened needles with one central bud, not unlike larch. The following year, however, the central bud extends in the normal way.

The second attempt at embedding wire in the flaccid trunk was better thought out. This time I used copper wire because of its superior rigidity. I gouged the channel even deeper into the trunk, allowing the wire to be forced in right to the center. I also used small hardwood wedges to hold the wire in place, guaranteeing that no amount of resin or manipulation would dislodge it. After only three months, the inevitable resin deposit is beginning to cover the wire rather than accumulate beneath it, suggesting that this time the device will work properly.

THE LESSON

The first time I attempted to embed wire in the flaccid trunk my workmanship was, frankly, shoddy. I didn't realize how much resin would be deposited beneath it. Neither did I anticipate the force this resin would exert on the wire. To compound the problem, I had neglected to anchor the wire by inserting it into the stable woody base of the trunk.

At the second attempt, I was far more con-scientious. I used copper wire for added strength, cut the channel much deeper and drilled a one-inch (25mm) hole into the base so the wire could be firmly anchored. I also used hardwood wedges to hold the wire in place. These wedges are moved every few months to allow the callus to form uniformly throughout the length of the channel. A tedious task, but eventually it will pay off.

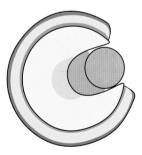

The original channel was too shallow and the resin deposits (shown here in orange) forced the wire out.

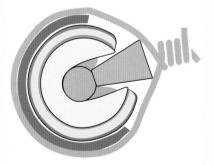

At the second attempt, I deepened the channel and held the wire in place with hardwood wedges.

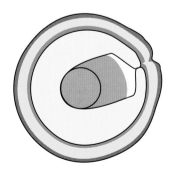

Once the channel has finally healed, the wire should be held permanently in place.

groove, holding it in place with cut-paste as a temporary measure. Then I bound wet raffia tightly around the trunk, covering the cut-paste and filling in any gaps between the raffia and wire with short wire offcuts in order to keep the strand as deep in the groove as possible.

Mistake number two: I should have used copper wire instead of aluminum. The aluminum wire was certainly strong enough to do the job, but copper wire would have been it better. Copper would also have had enough strength to allow me to introduce bends in the trunk without the need for additional wiring. At least the trunk could now support its own weight—or could it?

Mistake number three: I began the groove at the very base of the trunk. What I should have done was to drill a hole down into the woody core of the roots and insert the wire into this hole to anchor it. Although the trunk itself was now more rigid, there was a weak point at its base, where it wobbled frighteningly. Whatever, the job was done and I certainly didn't want to risk any further damage by doing it all over again.

Two years later, when I removed the raffia the wound had still not healed. It seems that at this small scale things don't work quite as fast as they do on more substantial trees. The healing process was pitifully slow because the trunk bore comparatively little foliage and was thickening imperceptibly slowly. This meant that it wasn't healing quickly either. But it certainly hadn't shown any reluctance to produce masses of resin. The sides of the channel had become encrusted with hard white deposits that had covered the cut-paste in some places and forced it out of the channel in others. This didn't look good so I scraped away at the resin until it was almost all removed and I could see the wire. I applied more cut-paste and rewrapped the trunk—this time using a tight binding of strips of black plastic cut from a refuse sack. Why? Because I was sick of staring at bright raffia and black plastic is less obtrusive. Surely another two years would do the trick....

Mistake number four: I should have known better. Another two years further down the road, when I removed the black plastic, I found I was back to square one. The original resin deposit had pushed the wire out far enough for the healing callus to grow under it in places. There was some new resin deposit but not as

much as before. And there was still that wobbly base.

So almost four years after starting the operation, I ripped out the wire and did the whole thing again—properly (I hope!). I ground out all the resin and deepened the channel. I allowed the wood to dry for a few weeks, and noticed no new resin appearing, even though it was late spring. Things looked more promising. This time I inserted slightly thicker copper wire—pushing it into a hole I had drilled in the woody root core to stabilize the trunk base. This time I decided not to fill the channel with cut-paste because I have a feeling that covering the bare wood and the edges of the channel encourages resin. But I did take one additional step. I used hardwood wedges and wire ties at 2" (50mm) intervals to hold the wire firmly in place. This is

The first styling. Although I was fairly pleased with the result, the almost-horizontal section of the thinnest trunk began to bother me. I was also unhappy with the foliage arrangement on the cascading trunk—it was too heavy and lacked the horizontal emphasis of the other branches. This destroyed the visual energy of the sweeping crescent shape that the rest of the tree described.

After my second styling session the image appears to represent an altogether larger tree. The right-to-left movement is consolidated and the crescent-shaped sweep described by the foliage masses is greatly enhanced. Although the central and lower masses still need further refinement, there has been a significant improvement to the overall design.

Notice how subtle changes in viewing angle alter the feel of the composition. Each time the tree is turned a few degrees clockwise, the crescent becomes more pronounced and the image becomes more dramatic, wilder and more windswept.

REDUCING NEEDLE LENGTH

The needles on a full-size Scots pine are 2" – 3" (50 – 75mm) long. We want to shorten them to around one inch (25mm) or less, but how?

Limiting the nitrogen content of the fertilizer is one tool at your disposal (*see page 96*). Although this alone won't reduce needle size by much more than twenty percent, it will reduce the vigor of needle growth in general, making the tree more responsive to the other half of the equation.

As the needles extend, reduce watering to a minimum—just enough to keep the tree alive. (In rainy weather, put pines under shelter or cover the soil with plastic.) Scots pines (most pines, in fact) are very drought tolerant, but don't let that tempt you into foolhardiness— you still need to water, but less often, wetting the soil through without soaking it.

Continue withholding water right through the candle-pinching phase, monitoring the tree's behavior. If growth appears to stop completely, water thoroughly a couple of times, and it should soon pick up again in a day. By mid- to

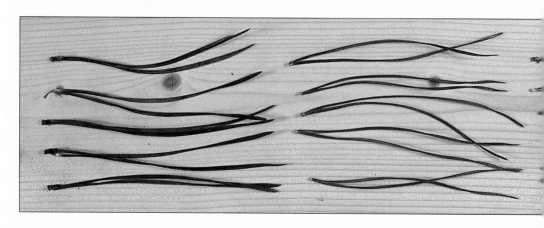

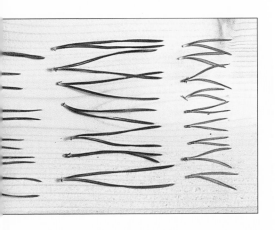

late summer, the needles will peel away from the stem and begin to darken. The change of color indicates that the needles have set and will grow no more. Only when the needles have reached this stage should you resume normal watering.

Remember that this technique only reduces the size of the needles that are currently emerging, not the existing needles nor those that will emerge the following year. To achieve uniformly small needles, water must be withheld during early summer each year.

as ugly as the raffia, but at least it's a different kind of ugly! There's now no way that the wire can move. Whether it is finally held in place by the callusing or by more resin is immaterial—so long as it stays put!

One style? Two styles? Three?

I began training soon after my first attempt at inserting the wire in the flaccid trunk. The tree was clearly ready for it, with hundreds of new buds on surprisingly old wood. The needles were short and dense with a good, rich color. The tree was ready, but was I?

The design problems associated with this tree were among the most perplexing I have ever encountered. In my mind's eye, I could plainly see a windswept literati style in the tallest trunk, with its lofty, arching posture and bowed crown. There was also some sort of sinuous semi-cascade style lurking somewhere in the lower trunk. But my precious middle trunk...? It was obvious that creating a single-style clump was out of the question; there was no way the trunk lines could ever be brought into harmony with each other, so I had to think of an entirely different approach.

Being a stubborn old goat, I was determined not to lose the middle trunk. Even so, I tried to

This practice is really only appropriate on fully developed bonsai. Small needles mean small food factories for vigorous growth. Developing pines need all the vigor they can muster for branch development and back-budding, so they should be watered normally.

A UNIQUE POT FOR A UNIQUE TREE

The final part of all bonsai compositions is the pot. In this case it was another difficult decision. My first instinct was to use a rustic crescent pot, but I decided against that on the grounds that it would be too prominent and would dominate the rather understated tree. Since the tree's image and lines are simple in spite of its structural complexity, a simple pot would be more suitable.

A further consideration is the implied natural history of the tree. Clearly it is a high-mountain tree, battered and blown by strong winds and sun. With a tree like this, a formal, refined pot would be incongruous, so I decided on a more rustic container. The current pot, which I think is ideal, was hand-built by Dan Barton to my design. He used a wonderful, earthy glaze with the look of rusty iron about it that suits the tree perfectly.

visualize the possibilities without it. Ironically, it was there that I found the solution to my problem. The upper and lower masses of foliage strongly suggested a crescent-moon shape, influenced by the trunk lines. This appealed to me a lot—it was unusual, it was exciting and it was not entirely unbelievable as a tree. If I could devise a way to manipulate the thin central trunk so its foliage reinforced this form, I might be onto a winner. This was going to be something different—the dynamic of the image was not going to be the trunk lines, as would normally be the case with this type of material, but would be derived from the line described by the positions and shapes of the three masses of foliage.

It took several attempts to get the movement of the thinnest trunk to work in a believable. treelike way. The first attempt created a horizontal section that I hadn't noticed until American bonsai artist Jerald Stowell pointed it out to me when I was showing him some photographs. From that point on it screamed at me! It jarred the eye and just had to be changed. The lowest foliage mass was also rather too heavy, and it curved back toward the pot, destroying the dynamism of the crescent I wanted to achieve. The upper canopy had a branch that swept back down the right side of the trunk.

Although I liked this branch, it also had the effect of diverting the visual energy from the crescent shape.

Having made these further adjustments I was much happier with the overall image. The lower foliage mass was still a little too heavy and all the branch outlines needed—and still need—to be smoothed and tapered to finer edges. Now that I can start reducing the needle length and cutting back to new adventitious buds as and when they appear, these refinements are possible.

Of all the species I have worked with over the years, pines are the most difficult to control and maintain as a static image. The new candles always grow vertically, regardless of the orientation of the bud from which they emerge. No matter how severely you pinch, they will always extend. When the old needles are removed annually, new areas of naked twig appear. Once a satisfactory image has been achieved, a constant annual strategy of reworking the outer areas becomes necessary, requiring patience, dedication and not a little ingenuity.

I can't help wondering what this pine will look like in a decade or so. I have a feeling it's going to be one of those trees I'm constantly tinkering with, never entirely satisfied. But that's bonsai!

Highland magic

SCOTS PINE FROM NORTH OF THE BORDER

Pinus sylvestris (Scots pine)

There are no rules for dealing with yamadori of this nature. You're free from the constraints of convention, so you can allow your imagination to take control.

IN THEIR NATIVE Scottish highlands, the pines grow in weird and wonderful ways. Seedlings weave their way through the long grass, heather and bracken to find light. As the vegetation is compressed by rain and snow, its weight also compresses the young pines. Eventually, some pine seedlings will find their way into the daylight and begin to grow more vigorously. What might appear at first glance to be a normal, shrubby young pine is, as often as not, quite old, and growing on an incredibly contorted trunk. Years ago, these pines were disregarded as bonsai material because they didn't fit conveniently into any recognized bonsai style. But nowadays, they are highly prized for the creative freedom and challenges they offer the more adventurous bonsai artist.

My good friend and student David Prescott (an up-and-coming bonsai teacher in his own right) had access to an area where he could collect some pines with the blessing of the landowner. On one of his frequent visits to my studio, David presented me with one of these magnificent pines, an outstanding gesture for which I will always be grateful.

This pine was, indeed, a challenge because it had not one, but two equally contorted trunks. Both trunks had interesting features in their own right but they just didn't seem to work well together. For two years I pondered over which

March 2000. Three years after collection, this contorted pine has been growing well in my garden for two years and has gained sufficient vigor to withstand the stress of replanting. This will also give me the opportunity to adjust the planting angle and revise the vertical and horizontal axes of the two trunks.

COLLECTING WILD PINES

Although I've only collected a small number of pines, I haven't lost one yet! David Prescott, who has more experience than I, also has an excellent success rate, as do others who follow the same practice. Between the two of us, we put together the following advice.

Recuperation

• Take as substantial a root ball as possible and wrap it very tightly in plastic sheeting and packing tape. Retain the flora growing in the root ball (apart from dandelions and other obvious weeds). This flora forms part of an ecosystem that the pine also plays a role in. They may share mycorrhizae *(see page 153)*, or some may influence the nature of the nutrient or trace element content of the local soil.

Subterranean organisms certainly do have a significant effect on the ability of plants to survive stress such as transplanting. These organisms, in turn, can depend on the local plants for their success. In simple terms, don't break the cycle until the pine is accustomed to living on its own new root system.

• Plant the pine in a large container using a very open, gritty soil with some coarse, acidic, organic matter—chopped fresh sphagnum moss is the best.

Water the soil with whatever you wish in the way of magic potions, but water it well, and don't feed until the buds begin to elongate. Cover the soil with a thick layer of live sphagnum moss, working it between the plants growing in the original soil.

• Semi-shade aids recovery. Placing several trees close together, so the branches interlink, creates a cool micro-environment for the roots beneath, not unlike the one they have just been robbed of. Mist as thoroughly and as often as you can. Feed gently at first, using fish emulsion as a foliar feed. Follow with fish emulsion in the soil and progress to meatier feeds (preferably organic) when the candles have opened. Concentrate the fertilizer on the new soil to draw out more new roots.

• Don't pinch candles during the first year. If growth is still weak in the second year, only pinch the more vigorous candles. Do no major pruning or bark stripping and certainly delay wiring until the tree is growing vigorously—at least three years.

Bare-rooting

• Bare-root at the first replanting. Bare-rooting eliminates the subterranean microenvironment that the tree was accustomed to, so this should only be attempted once you are sure the tree has produced sufficient new roots in the new soil to sustain itself in that environment. This probably means that the tree actually is sustaining itself on these roots. This being the case, the old soil is of no use to the tree because there are few, if any, active roots growing in it.

The old soil will eventually become lifeless and will set like concrete. Bare-rooting is, therefore, essential, and the sooner the better. Rather than hacking at the soil with a rusty root hook, hose the soil away. Help it along with a wooden stick, perhaps, but never, ever, use a multipronged root rake—or root ripper, as they would more appropriately be called.

• The major benefit of bare-rooting is that the new soil character and consistency will be uniform throughout the container. This helps promote even root development on all sides; ensures uniform drainage rate; gives you precise control over the moisture content of the entire soil mass; and enables you to feed all sides of the tree equally (or otherwise if you should so choose).

• Use the same soil formula as before, but this time the sphagnum moss is less important because there are already ample good roots—otherwise you wouldn't be doing this. Save some of the first soil mix to reintroduce near root tips. This will contain the spores and resting hyphae of the mycorrhizae that followed the roots from the old to the new soil after the tree was collected, as well as any other beneficial micro-organisms.

There's no need to worry about transferring harmful organisms in salvaged soil, because if the tree has been healthy in it so far, there clearly weren't any.

ABOVE: In the Scottish Highlands, the pines growing on open hillsides become contorted into bizarre shapes as they weave through the heather and bracken in search of a route to daylight. The sweeping curves and "elbow" bend of this trunk present an exciting challenge.

ABOVE RIGHT: The upright trunk sports fascinating jins that echo the natural movement of the trunk itself. Pine jins are brittle, unlike junipers or spruce, so great care is needed when cleaning them.

RIGHT: When viewed from the back, the best jins on the upright trunk are hidden, and the movement of the lower trunk is less pronounced.

SPHAGNUM MOSS: FIRST AID FOR ROOTS

Sphagnum moss (alias bog moss, long-fiber moss) was commonly used until the Second World War to dress wounds. It seems to have some magical properties that the roots of most plants also love. Mixing a generous amount of chopped, fresh sphagnum moss in with the soil greatly increases the speed and quantity of new feeder root production, giving the tree added vigor and improved color. The moss must be fresh and still alive to get the best results (the same applies for air-layers). Old moss that has turned brown and lifeless still helps a little but nowhere near as much.

Laying a generous blanket of sphagnum moss on the surface of the soil of newly collected pines keeps the soil moist and has a significant effect on the recovery rate. New feeder roots develop closer to the trunk, which is ideal, and they spread through the interface between moss and soil at an alarming rate.

One problem is that garden centers don't begin to stock sphagnum moss until the hanging basket season begins, which is after the repotting season ends! Nevertheless, it's worth grabbing a large bag while you can. You can keep the moss alive for a year or so by putting it in a clear plastic bag and storing it outside in semi-shade. So long as the moss gets light and remains wet, it will live until you next need it.

At first glance this looks like a photograph of a woodland floor, but in fact, it's the surface of the soil of newly collected pines. The micro-environment created by the moist, living sphagnum moss maintains perfect conditions for recuperation.

trunk to use. I even considered grafting some seedlings at the base of one of them to provide it with a new set of roots before severing it. Then, my natural fascination with multiple trunk styles took over—perhaps if I really tried hard one last time, I might be able to find a way to use both trunks in an integrated and harmonious composition.

The main problem was that the trunks were widely spaced—at about a 90º angle. One of them was lying flat on the soil and the other was virtually upright, at least at its base. Right angles are always uncomfortable in bonsai design, but when they align on the horizontal and perpendicular planes, they are downright painful to the eye. Clearly, the planting angle had to be changed, and repotting time was the natural opportunity to investigate the possibilities. In fact, I begin almost all my bonsai design projects in late winter or early spring, when I can bare-root the material and examine the root structure. Once replanted at the correct angle, the task of visualizing the design options becomes much easier.

While on the subject of bare-rooting bonsai material, I firmly believe that all trees, of whatever age, species or origin, must be bare-rooted at least once before being planted in a bonsai container. Thereafter, they should be bare-rooted every four or five years to guarantee a uniform soil structure throughout the pot.

I repotted in March 2000. When I told David Prescott that I had bare-rooted this pine only three years after he collected it, he was stunned that I could be so reckless. But he began to see the light six months later when it was growing with more vigor than ever in its new, uniformly structured, free-draining soil.

Murphy's Law

Murphy's Law states that whatever can go wrong will go wrong—and so it was with the nebari on my highland pine. I had hoped that the bulk of the active roots would be tucked under the prostrate trunk, but they were, in fact, on the opposite side. This meant that I could only tilt the tree by about ten degrees. Nevertheless, this was enough to eliminate their awkward horizontal-vertical axes. I also twisted the tree slightly to show more of the movement in the prostrate trunk.

I pruned no roots whatsoever. Because the

March 2000. Before I could do any design work, the planting angle needed to be decided, and this could only be done satisfactorily by bare-rooting the tree. Bare-rooting also ensures that, in the future, the roots will have a uniform soil in which to flourish. Note the tuft of new roots growing from the pruned root stub on the left.

March 2000. Now planted at its new angle, in a narrower but deeper box, the horizontal/vertical emphasis of the trunks has disappeared. I have removed one branch on the top right. This branch was clearly too long to be useful, and removing it at this stage reduced the demand on the roots, allowing the remaining branches to have a greater share of the available nutrients.

tree had been planted in a wide, shallow box, the new roots that had sprouted from the cut ends of the old roots had spread out evenly. More new roots had grown from the base of the trunks, just below what would be the visible nebari. By using a narrower but deeper box, I was able to accommodate all the roots with no problem. By the time this tree is finally planted in a bonsai container, there will be far more roots, and I will be able to reduce the volume without risking damage to the tree.

I waited until July 2000 before attempting any styling, by which time I was confident that the tree could withstand reasonable manipulation. There's little point in rushing and risking the loss of branches or even the entire tree.

Preparation

The key to successful styling of pines is in the preparation. First, all the older needles should

Whenever I'm asked what the best time is to wire Scots pine, I always say August. "Oh, why's that?" "Because the sun's hot, I can work on the patio in my shorts and the warm resin smells so good...."

August 2000. After one season's growth the pine has now more vigor and better color than it has had since collection. This is testimony to the advantage of bare-rooting and replacing old soil with new. Although the pine has grown well, the overall bulk of foliage doesn't seem to have increased much. This is because during April and early May all the long three-year-old needles were shed—a natural process at that time of year. The new needles are more prolific, but shorter.

My friend, student and benefactor David Prescott. Since he was generous enough to give me this pine, I thought it only fair to allow him to share the pleasure of plucking the old needles one by one.

A typical pine twig before needle-plucking. There are four types of needle, each with a different story to tell. The shorter, lower needles grew in 1998. At this time the tree was still recovering from collection a year earlier. In the next tier, the needles are much longer. By the time they grew, in 1999, the pine had fully recovered and was clearly well rooted in the new soil around the original root ball. Above these, there is a short section bearing very short needles. Rather than being an indication of poor health, these needles were produced on a second flush of growth in July 1999—something that happens only on healthy, vigorous pines. At the very top are the current year's needles, which are a good color and length.

The same shoot after needle-plucking. All the old needles have been removed, apart from two pairs at the base of an embryonic lateral shoot on the right. These were allowed to remain because plucking them would damage the bark and could easily cause the delicate new shoot to abort.

TOP: Before needle-plucking. The blue-gray needles are typical of Scots pine and one of its most endearing features. As you can imagine, wiring such heavily laden branches would be a nightmare.

ABOVE: After thorough needle-plucking, only the current year's needles remain. Now, wiring can begin.

be plucked out, leaving eight to twelve pairs of needles at the tips of each shoot. The number of needles remaining depends on the vigor of the shoot and the season. Weak shoots should have more needles left than the stronger shoots to balance the vigor. If you are wiring before the candles extend, you can afford to remove more needles than if you wire after the candles have fully matured. It's not wise to wire while the candles are extending or before they have matured because they are very fragile during this period and easily break away at the base.

When plucking out the needles, keep a look out for emerging buds. These appear between pairs of needles and can be difficult to spot. Wherever there are emerging buds or small, weak shoots, leave a few pairs of needles at the base to protect the buds and to remind you not to wire right over them.

The next stage is to cut or break off all the old pruning snags, which make wiring difficult. I find that the methodical approach is better than preparing the branches as I wire because it allows me to become more familiar with the tree and all its idiosyncrasies. On a large pine this can be a tedious task, but it does have its therapeutic value as well. Besides, if you think this is boring, wait until you start wiring!

BLIND SHOOTS

Pines frequently produce blind shoots—shoots that don't have terminal buds. These usually appear in weak areas or on inner branches that receive little light. Under normal circumstances these shoots would abort after a year, or two at the most. However, the cumulative effect of needle-plucking, pruning and wiring changes their circumstances.

When preparing pines for styling, retain these blind shoots but don't pluck off any of their needles. The chances are they will sprout buds somewhere within the next year. If not, they can always be cut off later.

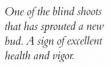

One of the blind shoots that has sprouted a new bud. A sign of excellent health and vigor.

The styling process

Even at its new planting angle, the two trunks of this tree still caused problems. The line from the "elbow" bend in the now-cascading trunk, back toward the base and up into the upright trunk, forms three sides of a rectangle. At first this is barely noticeable among the jumble of foliage, but I realized that this would become exaggerated once the foliage was positioned and refined. I tried turning the tree clockwise, but this made the fault even more prominent. Turning the tree fifteen degrees counter-clockwise, however, had a dramatic effect and instantly eliminated the problem.

Only one branch was removed to balance

TOP: After five hours of careful needle-plucking, the pine can now be worked on efficiently. The central portion is more laden with foliage than the extremities because of the straight branch that is growing toward the top right.

ABOVE: The unnecessary branch has been removed. Now the foliage is more evenly distributed, ensuring that all parts will have more or less equal vigor. The strips of card on the soil are to indicate the eventual soil level.

RIGHT: Stage one. The major bends in the trunks have been achieved by employing tourniquets. From this angle, which is my preferred front, the uncomfortable right angles between the two trunks are *no longer troublesome. I used black dyed raffia to bind the trunks and heavy branches before wiring and bending. Imagine how dreadful this tree would look if I had used natural-colored raffia!*

ABOVE: The copper wire tourniquets that I used to pull the trunks into position. If the anchorage devices are well padded, the tourniquets can remain for many years without damaging the bark.

RIGHT: Stage two. Every branch, twig and shoot has been wired. The thicker branches have been bent to maneuver the three areas of foliage into line.

Part of the cascading trunk had become swollen as a result of bearing two opposite branches at some time. Creating this small shari on the underside made this section appear thinner and exaggerated the movement in the trunk line—an added bonus.

the bulk of foliage on the cascading trunk with that on the upright one. Now I had to bring the two rather different trunk lines into harmony. The upright trunk had wonderful jins but the cascading trunk had none. This didn't bother me because it seemed natural that an environment that forced a trunk to cascade would also wreak havoc with any trunk that disobeyed. However, the top section of the upright trunk seemed to meander off into space a little too defiantly for my liking, so this had to be pulled

down and to the right with a tourniquet. This seemed to work well, but now the cascading trunk was a little too wayward. Now this needed an even stronger tourniquet to bring it under control.

Before attempting any movement of the trunks or thicker branches I bound them with raffia—dyed, of course. This black raffia, available from craft stores, blends with the bark and is far less visually obtrusive than the natural creamy white color.

LEFT: *After the first styling session in late July 2000. I tried to treat each trunk as a separate tree because I like multiple-trunk bonsai. However, in this case something is wrong, and I think it's in the canopy of the upright trunk....*

BELOW: *Wrapping paper around the apex isn't intended to be a final solution, but it helps gauge how the tree might look if the apex were removed. Not good.....*

BOTTOM: *Creating space in the upper of the two apices helps a little by reducing its visual power, but it's still not quite there. Eventually I lowered the bottom branch of the upper canopy to reduce its visual power (see overleaf). It now also relates far better to the foliage on the cascading trunk. That's it—for a while, at least!*

My working method usually involves introducing the major bends in thick trunks and branches first, bearing in mind the overall design I want to achieve. Once these are done, I wire the entire tree—every branch, twig and shoot. Even if I strongly suspect that I may remove a particular branch, I will still wire it, because it may be useful when I finally get around to placing the branches. Cutting it off later and wasting the wire is far better that cutting off the branch too soon and wishing you hadn't later on! Once everything is wired, you can focus completely on the branch and foliage placement without constantly interrupting your thought process to apply more wire.

All the major branches should be positioned first, manipulating large masses of foliage into the right areas. By working all the major branches at the same time, it's much easier to make them harmonize with each other. If you refine the shoots on one branch before positioning the next, you'll find yourself trying to make all the other branches harmonize with the first. In the end, you'll probably have to reposition the first branch and adjust all the shoots—or start all over again.

Once you're satisfied with the positions of the main branches, you can move on to the secondary and tertiary branches, but continue to work on the whole-tree principle. When all these are done, you can finally position all the fine shoots, manipulating the buds and needles so they are evenly distributed all over the branch area, thus defining the foliage cloud.

This compartmentalization of the tasks—

Every shoot must be wired right to the tip, with the wire terminating in a loose loop around the base of the cluster of needles. This enables each shoot tip to be turned upward, keeping the underside of the branch clean and creating a fuller, more mature image.

preparation, major bends, wiring, and placement of branches and shoots—is a difficult discipline to follow at first, but it always leads to a better result in the end.

Thoughts on design

Pulling the apex and the right-hand extremity toward each other compacted the tree and immediately added scale, age and movement as well as a sense of harmony. Viewing the tree from below horizontal makes it appear more dominating—larger.

The rather bizarre shape of the top section of the upper trunk is echoed in some of the smaller branches and, more importantly, by the prominent jins. The angle and movement of the lower trunk is a good counterbalance to the open, pendulous branches.

But do the two trunks work together? Initially I left a space between the two canopies in order to define them as belonging to two trees. After a couple of weeks, I began to reconsider. Both trunks are part of the same tree, and this is clearly visible. Trying to make them look like two trees was futile and pointless. I remodeled the upper canopy and brought the lower part down so that it almost, but not quite, formed a continuation of the lower canopy. This I prefer, and this I shall live with—for a while.

I will wait two years before repotting into a bonsai container. The pine certainly won't be ready to exhibit for at least that long, so there's no need for untimely root disturbance. In fact, repotting too soon would retard development and make that final goal of an entirely satisfying image even more remote. If the upright trunk is strong enough by then, I'll introduce a narrow shari or two on the left of the section that's now covered in raffia. The central section has a swelling where there had once been a cluster of shoots. I'll also indroduce a slightly spiraling shari there.

NOW, HERE'S A THOUGHT...!

If this hypothesis is true, can there actually be a "correct" eye level? Or is this a chink in the armor of tradition through which the artist might thrust his creative blade?

The accepted convention is that the correct height at which to view a bonsai is with your eye level at around the middle of the section of trunk below the first branch—about where your eye level might be on a full-sized tree—the "natural eye level," so to speak. (This rule does not apply to literati, because the first branch is at the top!)

This is all very good—but where is the natural eye level for a cascade? They say that with the eye at the right level you can just see the soil surface and the rear edge of the pot, but does that—should that—apply to a cascade? I would say, definitely not. Sure, you could see a natural cascade from any angle, even above, but the natural eye level would be from below. At least, this would be the case if you were as close as your distance from the miniaturized version would imply. To see a wild cascade from any other

angle, you'd need to stand a very long way off—whichraises another question.

As far as I'm aware, cascade and semi-cascade bonsai are all near images, that is to say, images of trees viewed from relatively close. But is it possible to style a distant cascade in the same way as a distant group or a distant literati? What elements, visual or otherwise, define the perceived distance of the tree—species, size, density, negative areas? Probably all of them to some degree, but I also believe that the elevation, or viewing height, has a much greater part to play.

Elevation is a design tool that's only available to us in the cascade and semi-cascade styles. But because of the traditional bonsai artist's reluctance to peel himself away from convention, it has never been properly explored or exploited.

Scots pine

Summer 2000

30 inches (75cm) high (from rim of pot);
32 inches (80cm) wide.

Container by William Vlaanderen,
Bonsai Design, Holland,
added by digital photo-montage

Larch

IF I HAD TO CHOOSE one species to work on to the exclusion of all others, there is a strong possibility that it would be larch. Larch have all the attributes of other needle conifers but also offer dazzling autumn color. As a friend of mine once observed, "Larch are busy little trees. There's always something to be done." How true this is.

Unlike most other conifers, which have one or two distinct, brief growth sessions each year, larch continue to grow throughout the summer, so there's always pinching and pruning to do. Although arguably the most flexible of all species, larch take several applications of wire before the branches are set firm. The clusters of buds that form at the bases of regularly pinched shoots need to be meticulously thinned in winter, in readiness for the next season's growth.

Larch need special siting as well. Although tolerant of full sun in open ground, once in a container they prefer shade, at least in the hottest times of the year. However, to achieve the best autumn color, they need to be reexposed to full sun as soon as summer's main force is spent.

Tiny larch cones with their delicate scales persist on the twigs for two years before shedding their seeds.

The stonemason's tale

A SHORT STORY ABOUT A TALL ROCK

Larix Leptolepis (Japanese larch)

It is nature's way that horticultural viability and aesthetic quality should lead to the same result.

ALL BONSAI enthusiasts who have been at the game for a few years have spare seedlings or nursery plants that they know are really not of much use but that they haven't the heart to throw away. Believe me, in time you'll realize that the junk just has to go, but meanwhile, it does provide the opportunity to practice techniques and experiment with design. Plants are not the only things that seem to find their way into our backyards. For example, who hasn't brought home a perfectly useless rock from time to time? These, too, can provide us with toys to play with on lazy days.

One miserable, dull Sunday in early spring 1987, I was bored and looking for something to

do. I had finished all my repotting and pruning, so I turned to my junk corner for inspiration. I had a dozen or so two-year-old Japanese larch seedlings that might have worked as the beginnings of a forest, but no container to plant them in. While searching for a slab in the rock pile, I found a piece of Welsh metamorphic sandstone. These rocks aren't the most stable and had become split into geometric, architectural shapes by the frost. The piece I had in my hand fascinated me. It was about 20 inches (50cm) long and four inches (10cm) wide, with interesting angles and facets. "Just like a cliff face," I thought. "Perhaps I could plant a tree in it somewhere."

RIGHT: 1988. The inverted (rather than cascading) larch, one year after the initial training. I experimented with adding smaller, accent plants to make the composition more scenic, but I later realized that simplicity is the key to success.

FAR RIGHT: 1991. Three years later, and another accent plant. You can see how weak the lowest branches are compared to those higher up.

SUDDEN DEATH SYNDROME

When you begin working with larch and the first repotting time comes around, you lift the tree from the pot and your heart sinks. The roots are little more than a mushy brown mess! You cut them back, hoping to find roots that at least look like they're alive. You find none, so you cut back even further. Eventually, you decide that enough is enough—there's hardly a single root of any description remaining—so you repot and hope for the best. As often as not the tree will sicken, and you wonder why. Was it the soil? Was it the winter cold? Was it overwatering? No—in fact, it was because you cut off all those roots!

Larch roots naturally appear rotten during winter and early spring. Inside that mushy brown exterior there's a fine white filament which is the perfectly healthy root. Why or how the roots do this, I know not. Perhaps it's a means of protecting the roots from hard freezing—after all, these are the roots that would normally be close to the surface in the wild and frozen solid for much of the year. But what I do know is that many a larch has been lost through panic root-pruning.

To make a long story short, I spent the rest of that day creating a vertical channel in the least interesting side of the rock. I utilized the natural shapes as much as possible, but I had to resort to the angle grinder in places—much to the chagrin of my neighbors, who didn't appreciate the noise and the clouds of dust! I used car body-filler to join small pieces to the main rock to complete the channel and to fix the rock to another piece of sandstone that became the base. That evening I planted one of the larch seedlings in the channel, tying the roots in with thin wire fixed to wire loops I had glued to the edges of the channel. "Cascade!" I thought, so I bent the trunk downward, wired the branches out and went to bed.

Revelation

Several years passed, during which the ramification slowly developed—with the emphasis on slowly! I assumed that the soil volume was insufficient for more rapid growth. Around that time, I was thinking about the standard bonsai teaching that a tree should be roughly triangular

LEFT: *The roots are contained in a vertical channel that I cut in the rear of the rock with an angle grinder. I also made another channel (on the lower right in the photograph) to house an accent plant, but the composition was too busy. Now this space is available to the larch roots. The moss is difficult to maintain because it dries rapidly in warm weather. I have to replace it each spring and again soon after midsummer.*

ABOVE: *I bridge the top of the channel with some galvanized steel mesh to help prevent the soil from washing out when I water. Also evident in this picture is the undercutting at the top right of the channel. I had to do this in 1997 to accommodate the thickening trunk. One day the trunk will become so thick that the channel will no longer accommodate it, and I will have to undercut again. Eventually, I suspect, this tree will have to find another home.*

LEFT: *I used some of the slivers of rock that I had cut away to extend the channel upward. These are fixed with car body-filler, which sticks to anything and sets rock hard.*

127

Mother Nature is a far better artist than any human could hope to be. All we can do is try to mimic her perfection.

in shape. Well, this one was—albeit an inverted triangle. But the function of the triangle is twofold: to make the tree visually stable and to ensure that the lower branches reach out to receive light. In that case, I wondered, how could this apply to a cascade?

I looked again at my inverted larch—the decrease in vigor toward the lowest point, the uncomfortable and unnatural shape which literally looked like an upside-down tree. Somehow it just didn't seem to have the feel of a tree thrusting out from high on a cliff face. I put the theory to the test and rewired the branches.

Bingo! Suddenly everything changed. This was no longer a weak, flaccid sapling, but a strong, vibrant tree reaching out into space on sturdy limbs. What's more, the vigor of the lowest branch increased dramatically, virtually equaling that of the crown.

The lesson

When dealing with cascade or semi-cascade styles, you don't simply invert the tree. Trees have a natural habit of growing upward, or trying to. Branches that are shaded by others deteriorate and die. Cascading trees are molded into that shape by external forces—snow, rock fall, wind, etc. It is the continual battle between the tree's natural habit and the external forces that shapes the tree. Whatever disaster befalls a tree, if it survives, it will always return to the universal tree shape with a narrow crown and wider base. If you follow this simple horticultural principle, you will almost always satisfy the aesthetic requirements as well.

TIMING IS EVERYTHING

Larch are sensitive to the timing of repotting. Fall and winter are out—larch must be frozen in winter to survive, and the freeze/thaw cycle will do freshly cut roots no good at all. So it has to be early spring, and I mean *early!* In winter the buds are normally brown, perhaps with a red tint. As spring approaches they turn shiny gold. Repot now! If you delay until the gold begins to split and reveals tiny specks of green, you're into the danger zone. The more green there is, the more dangerous repotting becomes. By the time the buds have become tiny green "shaving brushes," repotting is almost always fatal.

FOLIAGE CARE

Larch are among the hardiest trees on earth, surviving extreme cold for long periods in winter, and growing in the extreme north and at great altitude, where the unfiltered sun beats down on them relentlessly all summer, but their leaves remain green and fresh. In spite of this toughness, larch foliage is surprisingly delicate.

Exposure: When grown in a container, larch need shade if their foliage is to remain unblemished. When exposed to hot sun, the needles scorch. They turn brown, starting at the tips and spreading downward. There's no difference between the foliage on your bonsai and a wild mountain larch, but there is a big difference in the root system and local microclimate. No matter how frequently larch are watered, scorching will occur as when the sun gets hot.

Manhandling: Larch needles are softer than those of any other hardy conifer. They bend so easily it's hard to imagine it would cause them harm. Don't be fooled. It's tempting to rewire larch in summer, when the image is at it's best, but you must resist. The tree won't come to any harm, but the foliage will look dreadful for the rest of the season. Even slight pressure on the needles will cause them to crush and they will turn brown. Do all your wiring in late winter, a few weeks before repotting. Bear in mind, though, that when the buds burst, the bulk of foliage will radically change the tree's appearance.

Even though I took as much care as possible when adjusting the position of this shoot, some of the needles still became damaged.

Larch, like all conifers, look better if all the downward-facing needles are pulled off. On smaller bonsai, this becomes even more important. In addition, larch buds can appear on the top, sides or beneath the shoots. Once the branch framework is established, all buds that face downward or sideways should be rubbed off, so that the underside of the branch remains clean and the branch framework doesn't become too congested.

Japanese larch

Summer 2000

**22 inches (55cm) high (including rock);
17 inches (43cm) wide.**

A silk purse...

TURNING TRAGEDY INTO TRIUMPH

Larix leptolepis (Japanese larch)

It's curious how much even the most bland piece of material can offer the bonsai artist once it has spent a few years on the back benches.

WHEN I HAD more time than I do now, I used to sow seeds every year and religiously pot them on each year in the hope that one day I might open a bonsai nursery. Sound familiar? As a result, most of my friends and family have gardens full of trees they never wanted but felt obliged to accept.

I kept a few plants for my own use, among them a few Japanese larch. One was planted on a pillar of rock (see "The Stonemason's Tale") and the other—well, that one just sat around in a large pot for heaven knows how long. It was almost ramrod straight but it had an interesting shape at the top of the trunk where the leaders had been nipped off every so often. I decided to air-layer this section of trunk and use it for a *shohin*, and to make a formal upright style with the rest. Oh, dear! The air-layer finally failed after two years and the top died. Not only that, but the tree had been jammed in with other plants for the duration, and all the branches on one side had also died.

I'm not sure whether it was sentimentality or miserliness that prevented me from throwing

The problem larch. You can see why I hadn't bothered to take this tree seriously before, but it's amazing what you can do when you have to!

it on the burn pile straightaway, but I didn't. In fact I kept on watering, feeding, pruning and potting the thing for six more years. Then I was invited to give a lecture/demonstration at the Royal Horticultural Society's bonsai weekend, which was held at Wisley Gardens in February 2000. I needed some material that would interest members of the public as well as regular bonsai enthusiasts, so nothing too fancy. For the first time since my failed attempt at layering the top, I took a long look at this larch's potential. During its six years of casual topiary, the formerly straight branches had ramified considerably. There was certainly more than enough there to be able to train in a complete branch structure and achieve that "finished" image that demonstrations demand.

The problem apex. The remnants of the failed air-layer. You can see the ring of nodes circling the deadwood where the root production had begun. I had snapped the top off in disgust years ago.

NEW JINS AND SHARIS THE OLD FASHIONED WAY

It's trendy these days to plug in the latest power tool and turn vast areas of wood to dust in the name of art. In the hands of an expert, power tools can be used to produce wonderfully realistic, exciting shapes and textures. But there are so few experts and so many power tools! Besides, not every project is suitable for the fast-fix approach. I've seen many potentially good trees ruined by ill-executed power carving when a more subtle approach would have achieved a far better result.

The technique is simple: Lift up a sliver of wood and slowly peel it along the grain as far as it will go—or until you decide it has gone far enough. As you peel the sliver past knots or jins, it swerves around them as it follows the grain. The more distorted the grain, the more movement will appear in the texture. You can make wide fissures, narrow cracks, leave some areas smooth—whatever pleases you. If you want deep channels—even hollows—just keep on peeling!

This method has three important advantages over power tools. First, it gives you much more control. Second, the result looks more natural, because it *is* natural. Third, as the wood dries it naturally cracks along the lines of the texture you have created—not across the lines of carved texture.

If you think power carving is a therapeutic and pleasurable exercise, try this and, I promise, you won't be disappointed.

The long shari on this larch was textured and shaped without the aid of any tool other than a penknife and a hand drill that I used to hollow the knots. After being treated with lime sulfur and exposed to the weather for a few weeks, the surface of the new shari is beginning to look very old indeed.

Incorporating the two ugliest roots into the shari turned them to my advantage. They not only add interest to the base of the trunk, they also distract attention from the other ugly roots! The fine fibers that were left after I had peeled the grain were burnt off with a jeweler's blowtorch.

The problem roots. The swollen, tangled nebari are a result of my failure to comb out the roots when I first potted the seedling. Now, of course, they're too thick to move, but they do have a certain character that could be exploited, perhaps.

SUMMER PRUNING

Development

Larch have two types of growth: extension growth and spur growth (see page 156). Spurs occur on areas that the tree has decided it doesn't want to extend, and they have only one terminal bud. If you remove this terminal bud the spur will die. If you shorten a two- or three-year-old branch—by cutting away all the twigs with extension buds, and leaving only spurs—the chances are that it will be years before many of the spurs extend (see page 137). Bear this in mind when developing branches.

Now for some good news. Just below the involuntary apical jin was a cluster of buds and shoots that would easily form a dense apical zone within one season. Areas like this only develop with time, and they make working on well-established material much more rewarding.

Maintenance

In summer, maintenance pruning on larch deals only with extending shoots, since all structural pruning should have been done in late winter.

At the base of each shoot, surrounded by a collar of needles, there will be from two to four basal buds. The ratio of buds to needles in the collar is roughly equal to the ratio of buds to needles along the extending shoot. The numbers vary according to the vigor and

If you're going to make a long shari, you might as well go the full distance! I deliberately shaped the shari to emphasize the slight curve in the trunk and to imply a twist at the top.

So far, so good, but what about the total lack of branches on one side? The trunk was too straight for a raft, too curved for a formal upright (I don't know why, because it was ram-rod straight six years before!) and too straight for a windswept style. There was the challenge, and there was the subject of my demonstration: how to create a balanced image when the tree has branches only on one side.

I prepared the tree beforehand by shaping the apical jin and making the shari. Let's face it, no audience wants to sit and watch someone peeling away flakes of wood for three hours, but I did leave a small section on which to demonstrate the technique. When I got home after the demonstration, I made a few final adjustments in the peace and quiet of my workshop and sat back to admire my work.

By the middle of June 2000—just four months after the initial wiring—the image was more or less complete. This is the joy of working with larch. If you wait long enough before beginning the training program, and you feed and prune your larch regularly, you will have all age of individual trees. By this, you can be certain that by cutting a shoot almost back to its base, you will generate more secondary shoots, even if you can't actually see the tiny embryonic buds. Trust me!

When you want a shoot to extend a little—to add height to a branch or to fill a vacant area—allow it some freedom and then cut back to two buds. Cutting back to one will only generate one new shoot, which won't result in increased ramification.

ABOVE: Typical larch twigs, showing spurs and extending shoots.

FAR LEFT: Emerging shoots can be pulled out. They will break just above the basal buds.

LEFT: The embryonic buds are easier seen from below.

BUD CLUSTERS

After many years of pruning extending shoots back to the basal buds, tight clusters of up to twenty buds develop. These begin to make the naked branches look ugly in winter, and they produce foliage that is so tightly packed, the needles become distorted.

Each time you cut a shoot back hard, two or three new shoots grow from the basal buds. These are also cut back hard and, in turn, produce two or three basal buds each. The clusters of buds are, in fact, the basal buds of many pruned shoots, all emanating from the same point.

If you study them closely, you should be able to make out which buds are grouped on the same shoot stubs. You can then cut away selected stubs, leaving just one. The buds on the remaining stub can then be thinned to two. This does leave a frighteningly large wound area, but it dries and heals quickly and the remaining buds grow nonchalantly.

After several years of maintenance pruning, healthy larch will develop clusters of strong buds, which are the basal buds of the pruned shoot stubs. These can mean trouble and must be thinned.

By working out which buds share common shoot stubs, you can reduce them to a more manageable number—with care and sharp, pointed scissors. Here, seventeen buds have been reduced to just six.

This pruning scar is too close to the shari. From the front it makes the trunk appear to have inverse taper. Next spring, I'll widen the shari to include the scar and improve the trunk line.

you need to train a full set of primary, secondary and tertiary branches.

The morals of this tale are several. One: No tree is ever entirely useless. Two: Time is your greatest ally. And three: If you can't see a solution to the problem, maybe—just maybe—it's not the tree's fault.

One area that still needs some attention is this section toward the top left of the shari. The wound will swell as it heals (they always do on larch) and this will create the illusion of inverse taper in that part of the trunk. Next year, I'll extend the shari to include the pruning wound.

Balancing the design

To create a balanced image from a one-sided tree, you must consider how negative areas (areas within the tree's perimeter but which contain no branches or jins) can act as visual elements in their own right. To achieve this, the negative areas need to be defined by positive elements on either side. In this image, the vacant space on the left is defined by the rear branch and the first true left branch.

The back branch is, in fact, a secondary of the lower right branch. The fork is hidden directly behind the trunk.

Follow the line of the shari as it swells to the left. Halfway up there's a jin, which directs the eye into the negative area, which is defined by the branches immediately above and below it. The curve of the shari and the tension created by the longer branches pulling toward the right give the negative area a positive function. The result is a perfectly balanced image.

MAINTAINING THE SHARI

The new callus rapidly encroaches onto the shari. At first it is bright green but by midsummer it begins to turn brown. This callus tissue needs to be cut back, exposing a new layer of wood every one or two years. Here, the bark at the edge of the shari has been picked away in flakes, to help disguise the cut edge.

Larch produce healing callus at an alarming rate—up to half an inch (12mm) per year. Naturally, this means that any sharis you might make are far from permanent. By the time the thick bark at the original cut edge has blended with the new tissue, the shari can be reduced to almost nothing.

To accelerate the disguising process, pick off flakes of bark along the edges of the shari.

Every year or two peel back all the new callus tissue, right back to its point of origin. It won't be as thick as the original bark, so it won't leave that stepped appearance. Continued practice of this technique will result in a natural layered appearance as new wood is exposed each time.

Japanese larch

Summer 2000

**26 inches (65cm) high; 17 inches (42cm) wide.
Korean container added by digital photo-montage**

Old man of the mountain

ANCIENT ALPINE YAMADORI

Larix decidua (European larch)

The lesson that "less is more" in bonsai design can be a difficult one to understand. Seldom are there opportunities to demonstrate the principle more effectively than with this larch.

We're very lucky in Europe. Since 1993, we have been permitted to transport plants across national borders without the need for phyto-sanitary certification or quarantine. Believe me—European bonsai enthusiasts take full advantage of this wonderful freedom!

THIS COMPARATIVELY ancient European larch (*Larix decidua*) is one of my most valued treasures. It's not particularly large, but the bark shows a level of maturity that's very rare on larch of this size in the U.K., where the conditions are more suitable for healthy, rapid growth. I quite literally stumbled across this tree in the European Alps, while my friend and fellow bonsai artist Salvatore Liporace was ear-marking sabina junipers for later collection. I could see what appeared to be a small larch to my left, and a smaller clump of bare larch twigs to my right, but the six-foot-long (2m) branch that connected the two was hidden in the grass. I caught my foot under the branch and ended up flat on my face and feeling rather less than dignified. I tugged at the branch, more through annoyance than curiosity, but this was reversed as soon as I saw the small clump of twigs move.

I couldn't believe my luck. Below these twigs was a bizarre trunk, with immense taper. Two small, old, but apparently healthy, branches emanated from the top. The long branch that had unceremoniously stopped me in my tracks originated from the base of the trunk and had, no doubt, contributed to its taper. The buds on the small twigs were on the tips of "spurs," which larch produce on branches that are onto-genetically mature and no longer extending *(see page 156)*. Some of the spurs on these twigs were over half an inch (12mm) long, indicating that the twigs were quite old. My heart began to pound as I tore away the surrounding vegetation to investigate further.

The trunk was very badly rotted on one side. Clearly the trunk had snapped off many years ago, ripping away a strip of bark from the remaining stump. Since there seemed to be a reasonable distribution of heavy roots around the trunk, and the ground was soft and peaty, the temptation was too strong to resist. The only tool we had brought with us was a saw, which at least enabled me to cut off the long branch that had ambushed me. Sticks, stones and bare hands carried out the excavation. I managed to collect a root ball about a foot (300mm) in diameter after sawing through the thick roots. Fortunately, Salvatore did bring some useful packing materials. We wrapped the root ball in a black garbage bag and bound it tightly with strong adhesive packing tape.

As soon as we returned to Salvatore's studio in Milan, I carefully unpacked the roots and began to wonder how I was going to get this baby home on a crowded plane! I reduced the root ball a fraction by pulling out some of the larger stones and trimming back the thick roots a little further. I then repacked the roots, binding them even more tightly than before. Packing the roots in this way held the loose soil firmly in place and avoided any further disturbance during transit.

The tree was still too big to take on the plane as hand baggage. The two remaining twigs were still flexible, in spite of their age, which I estimated to be around thirty years. I managed to tie both down to the trunk. Then I bunched all the laterals together and tied them to the trunk as well. I still wasn't sure how I'd get this past the airport security guards, but at least it was a more reasonable size. As luck would have it, my conspicuous hand baggage fitted in the over-

REVITALIZING LARCH

Larch are cantankerous blighters, and it's not always easy to get them to perform exactly as you would like. I've seen many larch bonsai that are ontogenetically very old insofar as they produce only spurs and no extension shoots *(see page 156)*. This makes further development of a newly wired larch bonsai almost impossible.

Because these spurs persist all along the branch, right up to the trunk, it's not possible to prune back to a juvenile section (larch will not produce adventitious shoots from old wood). A quite young tree can be locked in an aged growth pattern because the juvenile growing tips to the branches were pruned away, leaving only the mature-phase parts.

So if pruning won't help much, how can we rejuvenate the tree and alter the growth pattern?

It seems that the mechanism that controls this aspect of growth is a "whole-tree" phenomenon. It's not localized to zones of changed hormonal activity, such as at a pruning cut. In simple terms, the restriction of the roots, probable trauma during collection and subsequent pruning have unwittingly mimicked the physiological conditions that come with chronological aging—stress and slow root growth.

So we reverse the process as much as we can by planting the tree in a larger container and allowing the roots to run free for a few years while doing little or no pruning. The vigorous root growth will change the behavior of the entire plant, and it will revert to juvenile phase. Eventually, a high proportion of the spurs will burst into life and thrust out strong, extending shoots.

When collected, this larch was entirely covered in spurs, with no sign of recent extension whatsoever. During the first year there was no extension growth at all—nor had there been for many years before I collected it. Only two very halfhearted little shoots extended no more than three inches (7.5cm) in the second year. During the third spring, at least sixty percent of the spurs extended. The vigorous young roots growing from older, mature parent roots have changed the growth phase of the entire tree and caused an explosion of vigor.

head bin with a hair's breadth (12mm) to spare. My excitement was so great, I hardly noticed the not-very-witty comments of my fellow passengers.

Back home, I immediately built a large wooden box and replanted my new treasure in an open, gritty soil with some chopped sphagnum moss added, to encourage new roots *(see page 116)*. I threw in just about everything I could think of to help guarantee the tree's survival—Superthrive, humate stress-reliever, mycorrhiza inoculant, trace elements—the whole nine yards! It seemed a long winter that year, but by early March, those beautiful little brown buds had begun to turn shiny gold. All was well.

The larch came through without any significant die-back. Growth was very timid, naturally, but the tree was healthy enough. I left it untouched for three full growing seasons before attempting any work at all. Rushing the work would have involved a certain risk, which I was not prepared to take.

February 2000. After three years in captivity there is ample healthy new growth to train. In order to be able to arrange the branches so that the elbowlike bend in the trunk line would be visible, I tilted the tree by about fifteen degrees.

At this stage I was not entirely sure which side I prefered. From this side, more of the wonderful deadwood is visible.

LARCH SPURS

Each ridge represents one year's growth.

The evidence of five year's growth is hidden in the branch.

This spur is unusual. It has five terminal buds, rather than the normal one. This is a sign of renewed vigor. Last season the single terminal bud tried to extend but didn't quite make it. It did, however, manage to produce a few lateral buds. In spring, all these buds will open.

The spurs on mature-phase larch twigs normally only have one terminal bud. Each spring this bud opens to form a flat rosette of leaves, with the next spring's bud already formed in the center. In fall, when the leaves are shed, they leave behind a minute ridge that sits on top of the one formed around the spur the previous year. As this cycle is repeated year after year, the spurs gradually extend—in alpine conditions by no more than one hundredth of an inch (0.25mm) a year.

By counting the ridges you can calculate the age of the spur, therefore the age of that part of the twig. But you also have to consider the fact that the twig has thickened over the years. The "root" of the spur is in the center of the twig, not at its surface. You have to take this into account and "guesstimate" the number of ridges buried in the twig.

A rapidly thickening twig will bury the ridges almost as quickly as they're formed, so the visible spur will be relatively short. On the other hand, a slowly thickening twig will have comparatively longer spurs. The ratio of spur length to twig thickness can, therefore, tell a lot about the past growth rate of that part of the tree.

ABOVE: The texture on the lower shari was different from that at the top. This section had been buried in leaf litter and had decayed. You can see where the annual rings have been exposed. By comparing their average thickness with the thickness of the trunk, I estimate the trunk to be around sixty years old.

RIGHT: The beautiful patterns in the grain of the broken trunk seemed to hint that there had been two breaks several years apart.

First Steps

In February 2000 I decided the tree could safely be repotted. The original mountain soil was poor and full of small rocks. This was washed away with a high-pressure hose, and I could see the heavy roots for the first time. They were not pretty! One of them had died and the others were hardly in the classical Japanese mold. However, since the rest of the tree was somewhat "off the rails," I didn't think it mattered. In fact, freedom from nebari dictating the angle or style can create wonderful opportunities for more imaginative designs.

The deadwood areas were spectacular. It appeared from the patterns of the etched grain at the top of the trunk that the original tree had snapped off on more than one occasion, and with several years between. Carving such beautifully etched natural deadwood would be a sin—nature's skill can never be equaled by man. But one piece of carving was called for. I had to cut off the stub of the long branch that I had tripped over three years before. Rather than leaving an incongruously large, carved jin in such a prominent position, I decided to create a hollow. I shaped the rim of the hollow to appear as old and as natural as possible. I don't really see the point of carving fine detail in wood as soft as larch, especially when it's still fresh. As the wood weathers it cracks and splits, and the surface adopts a texture of its own making.

The calluses at either side of the base of the shari had long ago met and fused. It appeared hollow underneath, so I began poking about with a piece of wire. To my amazement, once I had raked out all the powdery remnants that the colonies of wood lice had left after dining on the sapwood, I discovered that the living xylem formed a hollow shell around a core of dead heartwood. The wood itself is only connected to the living tissue at the top. The original break had also killed the root directly below the shari, and the lower part of the trunk had been buried beneath decaying leaf litter for many years. Extensive decay was inevitable. Immediate steps were now necessary to halt this decay and prevent the wood lice from returning. I used a clear horticultural preservative that is harmless to plants—once dry! It's also harmless when wet, provided it doesn't penetrate the soil or come in direct contact with any unprotected live tissue (foliage, open wounds, etc). I used the standard tools for this type of job: small paint brush heads on pieces of bent wire, cotton swabs similarly wired, a pair of long, narrow tweezers for retrieving the above, and a modified atomizer with a custom-built extension tube for all the really inaccessible places. Once perfectly dry, lime sulfur can be applied as normal.

Design decisions

The first important decision was taken during repotting. At its natural inclination, the trunk was only about fifteen degrees from horizontal. Working with that limitation would have forced me to raise the foliage above the top of the broken trunk in order to develop it in different levels. The elbowlike bend would be hidden. In my view, that would destroy the whole essence of the tree, so I tilted the trunk by another fifteen degrees or so.

The second, more difficult, decision was selecting which of the two frustratingly similar branches to cut off. Why not use them both? Well, keeping them both would have demanded that one could remain a branch and the other must become a new leader. This would have made the finished bonsai larger and more complex. This, in turn, would have made the imaginary tree whose image the bonsai evoked appear less ancient and, ironically, smaller.

A most bizarre discovery! The trunk is a living shell around a core of dead wood, which is normal. But in this case there's a gap between the two that continues all around the trunk.

The stub of the branch that had ambushed me in the Alps. Even though it had no foliage and was around 5 inches (12cm) long, callus was growing over the cut end.

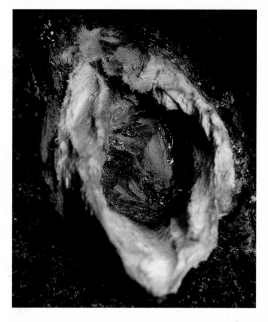

I removed the stub and carved a hollow. I don't bother with fine carving on soft wood such as larch. The weather does a much better job than I could. If you look closely, you can see that new callus is forming inside the hollow, between the darker heartwood and the sapwood. I'm still trying to figure this out!

139

From this angle you can see how neither of the branches follows the trunk line. What's more, the lower branch has a right-angle *bend near the trunk, where the original branch had broken off. The deadwood in this angle would be impossible to bend.*

ABOVE: The two crossing branches. Although the lower branch forks quite close to the trunk, its foliage begins further away than on the upper branch.

RIGHT: The old "cover one branch with a piece of paper" trick—but it works! Here you can see how, by using the upper branch, the transition from the original trunk to the new line is virtually seamless.

I cut off the lower branch just beyond the right-angle bend. I needed that "hook" to hold down the upper branch—assuming I could bend it that low.

Sure enough, after roughly shaping the jinned lower branch, I managed to prise the upper branch down and lodge it underneath—just!

After much deliberation, I finally decided to use the top branch. I had several reasons. First, it had a little more natural movement than the lower branch, which had an awkward sharp bend that included some deadwood near its base. Second, the transition between trunk and branch was smoother. Third, and most important, it began ramification and bore viable buds closer to the trunk. The only problem I could see was how to disguise the fact that the lower branch had been cut off. The most obvious and effective way was to leave a jin, but this would have interfered with the positioning of the remaining branch—or would it...?

I knew that the branches were still flexible, but I wasn't sure precisely how flexible. If the upper branch was flexible enough, I would be able to bend it down and hook it underneath the jinned lower branch—thus solving the problem of positioning the upper branch without damaging the bark at the same time. I couldn't test it first, so the only way to discover if my theory

OVERWINTERING LARCH

Larch are very hardy. If they don't receive several weeks of subzero temperatures they will deteriorate and eventually die. Having said that, the roots do need protection—not from the cold, but from temperature fluctuations. The constant freeze-thaw cycle that can occur on a daily basis when nights are cold but days are sunny somehow causes extensive root damage and can be fatal.

I leave my larch outside all winter in temperatures of between 10°F (–12°C) and –5°F (–20°C). To protect them against temperature fluctuation, I keep them in shade, in an area where the overnight frost lingers the longest.

ABOVE: Not the best nebari! It's essential to bare-root all collected trees at some point, to provide them with the maximum volume of good, controllable soil. Using an open, gritty soil at the first potting after collection makes it easier to remove the new soil to begin with, which avoids damaging the new roots.

LEFT: The roots wouldn't support the tree at the new angle, so I used a bamboo strut at the rear and pulled the tree onto the strut with wires attached to the box.

Never repot larch if you can see green in the buds. This is a crucial time for larch, and any disturbance is likely to kill the tree. Fall repotting is normally safe, but I prefer early spring.

worked was to do it. So I did it. It worked! Although, there were some frightening cracking sounds as the thick bark stretched and fractured under the strain. If I change my mind about the jin, I can cut it off and carve a hollow once the branch has set in position.

How to shape the jin was another dilemma. I could always carve it—that would be easy enough, but it would always look like it had been carved. Ripping strips of grain with pliers is usually the most effective way of creating a natural-looking texture, so I took this route. I was careful not to introduce too much texture or detail. Larch wood is soft and expands and contracts dramatically with changes in the weather, so fine detail is soon lost. It's best to create the basic shape and major fissures by hand and let the weather do the rest.

The engineering

My biggest practical problem was how to maneuver the remaining branch into position, and how to introduce some more movement into it without damaging the fragile, flaky bark. I solved this problem by passing a steel rod in front of the branch and lashing the bottom end to the nebari at the rear (for the time being) of the trunk—using the trunk itself as the central fulcrum. This pulled the branch back in line with the trunk, which was perfect! The pressure of the steel rod against the bark was cushioned with plenty of rubber padding.

A wire stay fixed to another root pulled the branch down further and introduced an extra bend. I found that by altering the point where the steel rod crossed the branch I could adjust

I prefer to support unstable trees by tying them to the container rather than wiring the roots into the pot. Wiring places additional stress on the roots and can cause significant damage if the roots are growing well. Visible ties can be tested periodically and removed or replaced easily. They can also be adjusted individually to fine-tune the trunk's inclination.

Larch should always be wired in spring, well before the buds open. Wiring when the buds have opened can damage the tender young foliage and seriously debilitate the tree. Wiring in fall or winter is often fatal to the tree. For some reason, larch just don't like spending winter with wired branches.

I pushed a steel rod down in front of the branch and lashed it to the heavy roots at the rear of the trunk. Using the trunk as a fulcrum, the rod levered the branch back in line with the trunk.

The pressure exerted by the steel rod against the trunk was considerable, so a generous layer of thick rubber padding was called for to protect the bark.

ABOVE: By pulling the branch down with a wire tie fixed to a heavy root, I was able to achieve the angle I wanted. Adjusting the position of the steel rod and the tension of the wire ties introduced more movement.

Once I had finished styling the tree, I returned to the jin and refined it a little by peeling away strips of grain.

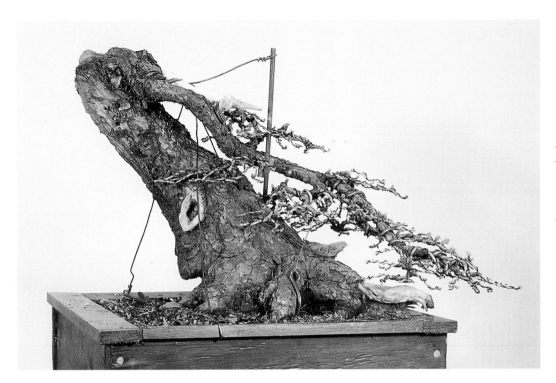

Initial wiring is complete. The image looks very thin, but this is the way with larch. Although they are deciduous, they have branch structures like any other conifer, not like other deciduous trees. Imagine, for example, how thin your favorite pine bonsai would look without any needles. In spring, the branches will be clothed in a layer of foliage at least an inch (25mm) thick.

the movement in the branch. A further wire tie held the top of the steel rod in its final position.

At its new angle, and without the support of the original stony soil, the trunk was unstable. A simple bamboo strut was sufficient to take the weight of the tree at the rear, and when I pulled the trunk onto the strut with wires attached to the box, the whole assembly became "locked" in position. After a few years the root system will be strong enough to support the trunk unaided.

Positioning the branches

Although I was desperate to carry on working this tree, I had the self-control to let it recuperate from the repotting, pruning, jinning and bending before doing any further work. "At least a year," I said to myself, as I grudgingly put the tree back on the bench. "Not likely!" I said to myself as I took it back again after three weeks. By then, the buds had begun to open. Clearly this tough little larch had bounced right through its trauma as if nothing had happened. But it was almost too late in the tree's cycle to begin wiring, so I had to act quickly.

Fortunately, larch are a dream to wire. They have the simple geometric structure of all the Pinaceae family but, being deciduous, don't require hours of laborious preparation. They are also the most flexible species I have ever worked with. Old branches bend easily, young branches can literally be tied in knots, although

I can't think why anyone would want to try it!

I wanted the branches to hug the trunk and emphasize the dramatic taper and 345° bend at the top. Keeping the foliage low and separated into wide, shallow and compact tiers would make the trunk appear even more massive. When wiring larch it's essential to understand that the spring foliage will add considerable bulk and density to the branches. Space must be allowed within each individual branch, as well as between the branches, to accommodate the foliage. In winter, the branches of a correctly wired and pruned larch will always look too thin and underdeveloped.

Future development

The dimensions and positions of the branches are more or less as they should be. All that needs to be done there is to improve ramification and fill in the sparse areas. I need to work on the roots, to develop a more efficient and compact structure that will support the trunk. I also need to be persistent in treating the deadwood inside the hollow lower trunk to prevent further deterioration. Of course, I need to find a suitable pot—or have one made. Most importantly, I need to make up my mind which side will be the final front. Although I have selected one for the time being, there are several that are just as exciting, and that work just as well with the existing branch layout.

143

THE ALL-ROUND VIEW

Let's take a look at the three design elements that combine to make a bonsai with several possible viewing angles, each with its own character and merits. As for which is the "best," that's a subjective decision. I've made up my mind for the time being, but it is highly likely to change!

• *The trunk*—This is massive and dramatic in its taper and switchback bend. It has tremendous power from all angles and, whichever way you look at it, offers exciting features.

• *The new trunk line*—This really sets the style of the tree. Although it is relatively thin, it has sufficient visual prowess to reverse the thrust of the main trunk.

• *The branch configuration*—To give this bonsai image perceived size I had to train the branches into several tiers. Height was limited, so the tiers had to be wide and shallow. My strategy of allowing free growth for three years had provided me with enough new growth to achieve this in all dimensions.

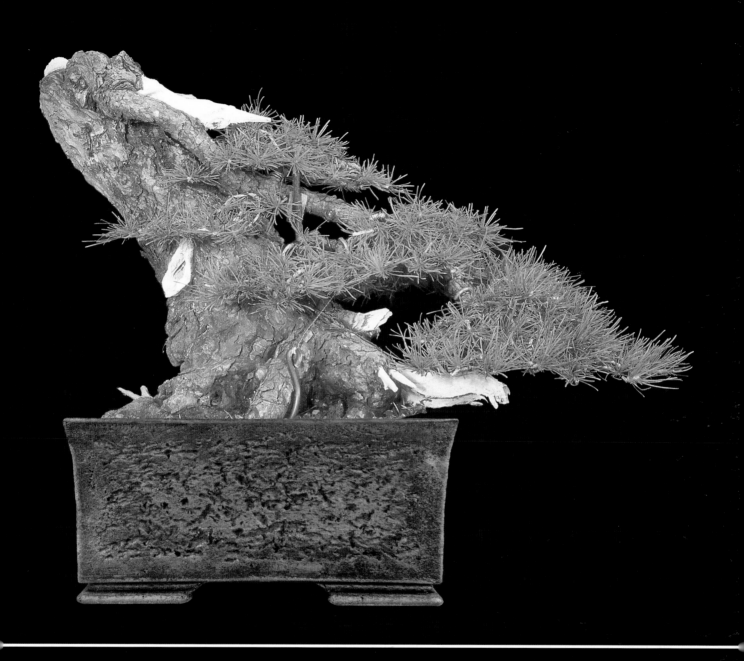

European larch

Summer 2000

13 inches (33cm) high (from rim of pot);
58 inches (14cm) wide.

Container by Dan Barton,
added by digital photo-montage

Appendices

Essays on the art and science of bonsai

The naked truth

THE DECIDUOUS CHALLENGE

MANY WESTERN bonsai artists I have spoken to express a preference for conifers, and some deny any interest at all in deciduous species. Perhaps this is a result of what I call the "demonstration syndrome"—the pressure for rapid results. It is certainly widely influenced by the innovative work of Masahiko Kimura.

It could be said that by specializing, the artist becomes more proficient in his chosen discipline and is therefore more able to challenge conventional artistic frontiers. On the other hand, there is always the danger that some aspects of bonsai may fall victim to fashion and become neglected or even disappear completely. Is it possible that the role of deciduous species in bonsai art could be under such a threat?

There is a clear distinction in mood and emotion between coniferous and deciduous bonsai—although neither is superior. But deciduous trees have an added dimension: the image profoundly changes with each season, and with it the spirit also changes.

In spring, tiny buds burst to reveal minute, perfectly formed leaves. The tree is vibrant with color and full of promise. In summer, when more heavily laden with foliage, deciduous bonsai are subject to more or less the same aesthetic criteria as conifers. In autumn we are rewarded by yet another dramatic change of character, this time a triumphant finale to the passing season.

But in winter the tree stands cold and naked, nothing can be hidden from view. The true souls of both the tree and its artist are exposed to the world's scrutiny.

Whether the tree is proud of its nakedness or shamed by it depends entirely on the competence and sensitivity of the artist who created it. When displaying a conifer in winter the artist says, "Look what I have done." By displaying a deciduous bonsai in winter he also says, "Look how I did it."

With deciduous bonsai, therefore, branch structure is of paramount importance. Branches trained in unnatural lines, merely to fill a space with foliage, are a symptom of the lust for rapid results, regardless of species. Although also unacceptable in conifers, at least such contrivances are hidden from view all year. You may know they exist, but the world does not. It is for each artist to decide whether he can live comfortably with this knowledge. But without foliage to conceal them, such unscrupulous branches will cause any bonsai to lose its integrity. Is the integrity truly preserved simply because the fault is hidden from view?

Deciduous species also offer just as broad a range of images and emotions as those offered by conifers. The shapes may differ. The "visual language" such as jin, shari, branch lines, color and texture may change. But the image of an ancient oak, as old as time itself, tortured by centuries of attack, or a thrusting maple, vibrant with joyful vitality, can fill your heart, stir your soul and sing just as sweetly as any conifer.

Deciduous bonsai cannot be rushed. There is no formula for producing a seemingly established image in one session. Deciduous bonsai must be created slowly, a combination of vision, forward planning and adapting what nature presents each cycle. Branches must be built, year by year, each new shoot guided by wire until the entire network is complete. They become brittle at an early age, so once the work has been done it cannot be changed. The ghosts of mistakes made many years earlier return each winter to haunt you.

The discipline of building branches in this way, the attitude of mind required to embark on a long-term project and, above all, the need for absolute integrity in your work, are all valuable lessons. Moreover, once learned, they serve to improve the integrity of all your bonsai, deciduous or coniferous.

European Hornbeam (Carpinus betulus) grown from a larger landscape tree.

An infatuation with elms

First encounters

I MUST HAVE been no more that three years old. The house my family lived in at the time had a hedgerow at the bottom of the small garden. I remember my mother panicking when I picked some bright red hawthorn berries and popped them in my mouth. There was no need for her to worry—hawthorn berries are harmless and not without some nutritional value. I also recall what I now know to be elm.

I was fascinated by the strange, corky bark on the twigs that broke off easily and tasted slightly bitter. I remember the coarse, bristly leaves, rough like my father's chin and covered in minute red pimples. When I started school I used to walk past more elm hedges, breaking off long shoots to play with on my way home—make-believe fishing rods, bows and arrows. Before long I knew which shoots and twigs would bend without snapping, which would let me peel away their bark to reveal that beautiful

Elms have a chaotic, twisted grain that carpenters exploit for chair seats and cartwheel hubs because it won't split. Old elms often shed bark to reveal this beautiful texture beneath.

smooth and slippery wood, and how to break off thicker twigs whose tough fibers were determined to frustrate me. I remember my curiosity at the brown liquid that oozed from fissures in the trunks of some trees.

During my early teens I spent much of my spare time in the local park, which was bordered by towering mature elms and the inevitable patches of elm scrub. One autumn, a large branch fell from one of the trees. No one was hurt, but the local authorities decided that the risk was too great. The following spring a dozen or more were felled. My sadness was more than compensated for by the opportunity to walk the trunk right to the top and clamber around in the massive branches before the chain saws arrived to dismember these poor dead giants. The trunks were all hollow—many filled with wet, coffee-colored granules of semi-decomposed heartwood. This must be what was oozing from those fissures in the trunks, I thought.

Spring was not the best time to fell these trees. Scattered around were hundreds of newly hatched rook chicks, flung from their nests and killed as the trees hit the ground. Their mourning parents circled in flocks for days, calling constantly in their grief. You hardly see rooks at all these days. Elms were their preferred nesting sites and few other species grow so tall or offer the same tough twigs to build their rookeries. Dutch elm disease killed more than just elms.

Elms for bonsai

In the Western hemisphere there are scores of species of elm, all of which take well to pot culture and respond reasonably well or excellently to bonsai training techniques. In Europe, wych elm (*Ulmus glabra*) and smooth-leaved elm (*Ulmus carpinifolia*) are commonly used, but they

Elm foliage:
Leaves collected from free-growing trees and bonsai.

FROM LEFT TO RIGHT:
Zelkova serrata;
Ulmus parvifolia
   (Chinese elm);
U. pumilla
   (Siberian elm);
U. elegantissima **X**
'Jaqueline Hillier';
U. procera
   (English elm).

have one drawback: they are both apically dominant. This means that after pruning or pinching, no matter how severe, only the one bud nearest the tip of the severed shoot is certain to sprout. The others will remain dormant.

ENGLISH-SPEAKING ELMS

Of all the elms in Europe, English elm (*U. procera*), alias Field elm (*U. campestris*), is by far the best for bonsai in all its aspects. It is remarkably similar in its foliage, bark and growth habit to the American elm (*U. americana*).

Both respond to pruning at any time of year by regenerating many strong shoots that will set in position within a few weeks after wiring. Both are also prolific rooters and begin to deteriorate if not frequently repotted. The roots are so dense and fine that they rapidly become a tightly woven mat that is almost impervious to water. All my elms (with the exception of the saikei in *Memories of Olde England*) are repotted annually. Almost all the fine roots are pruned away, leaving just a few on the thick storage roots. In order to achieve this annual purging of the root system, I wash all traces of old soil away with a strong jet of water from my garden hose. I save a little to mix with the new soil in order to reintroduce beneficial microorganisms that my largely inert soil doesn't contain.

These elms are not hungry trees. In fact, overfeeding often results in abnormal growth—either by direct effect on the shoots or indirectly by killing roots and allowing soil-born pathogens to enter. One such pathogen, as yet

unidentified, causes the leaves to become puckered and adopt a silvery sheen. The leaves and the terminal node of the shoot soon wither and die. Part of the shoot usually survives and lives on, but growth is severely retarded for a while.

MORE ELMS
• Jacqueline Hillier elm

Ulmus elegantissima **X** 'Jacqueline Hillier' is described as a slow-growing shrub, but in a bonsai container it grows as fast as almost any other elm. It's a fairly recent hybrid with great potential for bonsai because of its small, regular

Jacqueline Hillier elm in training. Very dense, very vigorous in the second and third years after repotting. This rather old specimen with an eight-inch (20cm)-diameter trunk was six feet (2m) tall when it was salvaged from a derelict garden four years ago.

149

ABOVE: Chinese elm
(U. parviflora)

RIGHT: Siberian elm
(U. pumilla) *in training*

In spring the tiny dark brown elm buds open to reveal minute, bright green leaves that sparkle in the sun—perfect in every detail, like a baby's fingernails.

foliage and very compact habit. If anything, it is too compact for the casual bonsai grower. The neat leaves are borne very close together either side of zigzag shoots, so close that they often overlap. When the following flush of growth begins almost every axillary bud will sprout, forming a flat herringbone pattern not unlike *Cotoneaster horizontalis*. Most of these will abort because of the dense overcrowding, but with constant selective pruning you can easily control which ones survive.

Jacqueline Hillier elm is much underused, and a lot of work is still needed to assess fully its potential as bonsai material, but thus far it looks very promising. One drawback is that the branches are extremely brittle—far more so than any other elm—breaking without warning just as you manipulate them into position.

• Chinese elm

Ulmus parvifolia is the most popular and common elm used for commercial bonsai production, if not the most common of all species. It has quick growth, tiny foliage, dense, fine twigs and an almost fanatical obsession with producing adventitious shoots from all parts of the tree. It is almost as hardy as the other elms discussed here and can be grown with reasonable success indoors as well as outside. The only tender part of the tree is the fleshy root system, which is easily damaged by the winter freeze-thaw cycle.

• Siberian elm

Ulmus pumilla is a native of the far north, as the name suggests. When grown in more southern climates its growing season is extended three-fold, and annual growth is phenomenal. The foliage is similar to Chinese elm but somewhat larger and slightly hairy. Branches are flexible and set rapidly after wiring. Siberian elm's reaction to pruning, however, is less than perfect. It will throw out the expected proliferation of adventitious shoots, but wounds are slow to heal. Often the surrounding bark will die back, leaving a much larger wound than the one you created. The bark is also easily damaged when wiring, and this, too, often dies back, sometimes resulting in the death of the branch. In spite of its extremely rapid growth in open ground, once in a container, the growth slows to the same rate as other large elms. The one pictured on the left increased in trunk girth from one inch (25mm) to over three inches (80mm) in one season.

• **Zelkova**

The common name of *Zelkova serrata*, Japanese gray bark elm, is misleading because it is no more closely related to true elms than plums are to pears. However, its close similarity in growth and habit justify its inclusion here. In fact, although I confess to being besotted with elms as bonsai, in the chapter "Close to the Edge" I explain why I chose zelkova rather than elm for one particular bonsai planting. Zelkova leaves are almost translucent when young, pale green and often edged with bronze or red. The shoots are slightly zigzag but not excessively so. Fall color varies from yellow to red, and can include all shades between. In all aspects of cultivation it is more or less identical to *Ulmus procera* and *U. americana*.

Problems with elms

Very few elms are ever attacked by aphids or spider mites, the bonsai grower's deadliest enemies. I have never experienced aphids on elms in over 25 years, but there are those who say

A tangled mass of fine roots fill the pot in less than one season. In damp weather the roots may emerge from the soil and creep along the surface before plunging down into the soil again. Most die on their first exposure to the sun.

WARNING:
Chinese elms regularly drop all their leaves after applications of systemic fungicides or insecticides. This is rarely fatal. Although some very young shoots may abort, the tree normally recovers after a few weeks—if a little weakened by its experience.

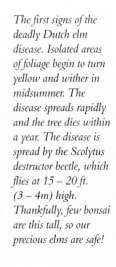

The first signs of the deadly Dutch elm disease. Isolated areas of foliage begin to turn yellow and wither in midsummer. The disease spreads rapidly and the tree dies within a year. The disease is spread by the Scolytus destructor beetle, which flies at 15 – 20 ft. (3 – 4m) high. Thankfully, few bonsai are this tall, so our precious elms are safe!

LEFT: *Pinching the new shoots too early in their growth phase, or too soon after feeding, results in these strange-looking shoots with no proper leaves for the first few internodes. Pinching forces the embryonic axillary buds to open before they have fully developed, while they are still empty shells. As the shoots extend, they carry the bud scales along with them to replace the missing leaves. Since bud scales are, in fact, modified leaves, there are axillary buds that can be used later at the point where they join the shoot.*

The trunks of mature English and American elms are frequently hollow and filled with an unpleasant brown fluid that oozes from cracks and old wounds, often leaving a permanent stain on the bark. Sometimes arborists will use concrete to block these gaps and insert a catheter to drain the fluid. This English elm is one of a pair growing alongside a stand of American elms opposite the State House in Boston, Massachusetts.

they have. Apart from the many types of harmless but disfiguring gall mites, which are endemic to elms all over the world, the main problems are thrips, leaf miners and black-spot fungus diseases. All these are easily and effectively treated with everyday garden chemicals.

The dreaded Dutch elm disease, which devastated indigenous elm populations throughout the West, rarely—if ever—attacks bonsai. They are usually kept way below the flight path of the scolytus beetle that spreads the deadly fungal spores.

Elms are prolific rooters, filling a pot with a tangled mass of fine roots in less than one season. In damp weather the roots may emerge from the soil and creep along the surface before plunging down into the soil again. Many of these die on their first exposure to sun, but some survive. By the end of the summer, the soil can become covered by a virtual carpet of dead fine roots.

Deeper in the soil, the roots become as dense as a coconut fiber doormat. Water takes longer to penetrate and, although the surface appears waterlogged, the soil below may be bone dry.

I routinely repot all my elms annually, regardless of age or size, and bare-root them every second year. If a year's repotting is missed, by the following June, I have to bore holes in the soil to allow the water to penetrate.

Tiny galls are a regular feature of most European and many American elms. Each species hosts its own particular mite that burrows into the leaf tissue and secretes a hormone which prompts the leaf to form the galls in which it lives. In midsummer the mites migrate down the leaf and into the axillary bud, where they spend the winter breeding. Some leaves can emerge in spring with over one hundred galls. Just imagine how minute these creatures must be for several leaves all to contain that many mites in one tiny bud. There is no known treatment for gall mites, but they are relatively harmless, so there's no need to panic. If they become really unsightly, pull off all infested leaves before they turn red in midsummer, and burn them. This will eliminate the mites before they migrate to the axillary buds and will prevent reinfestation next year. Before long, however, more will drift in on the wind.

Mycorrhizae

MICROSCOPIC MIRACLE WORKERS

THE TERM "mycorrhiza" (plural "mycorrhizae") is rather like the term "partnership." It describes an association, a relationship. If both parties to the relationship are compatible, and conditions suitable, they will both benefit; otherwise the relationship is of no benefit to either and it ceases. One party to this relationship is your tree, and the other is a microscopic fungus. The fungus forms a sheathlike structure at the root tips, through which it passes to the tree nutrients it has gathered from the soil in exchange for food the tree has produced through photosynthesis.

Almost all vascular plants benefit in nature from some kind of mycorrhizal association. Although mycorrhizae are by no means essential to the well-being of any plant, they are of tremendous benefit in less than ideal circumstances. For example, a tree planted in fertile soil with a good supply of readily available nutrients will already be growing at its maximum rate with maximum health, and so has little need of mycorrhizae. Indeed, as we will see later, mycorrhizal fungi would probably not survive for long in such conditions anyway. On the other hand, trees planted in marginal conditions would probably not survive without a mycorrhiza, and it is in these conditions that mycorrhizae will thrive.

This begs the question, "Is bonsai soil in a bonsai pot ideal or less than ideal?" The answer has to be yes. Bonsai containers provide marginal conditions for any tree, and it's only the dedication and knowledge of the grower that enable the tree to thrive. In a bonsai pot the roots are subjected to the extremes of temperature and regular drenching and drying. The soil is largely inert (Akadama, calcined clay, grit, pumice) and any nutrients are rapidly leached out with daily watering. These are exactly the conditions in which mycorrhizae can be of profound benefit.

ARE MYCORRHIZAE SPECIES-SPECIFIC?

Not as a rule. There are a few mycorrhizal fungi species that will only associate with one host species, but the vast majority have a broad range of potential hosts. Likewise, virtually all plants—and almost certainly all trees—are perfectly happy to form mycorrhizal associations with a number of different fungi.

A closer look

TYPES OF MYCORRHIZA

There are two major types of mycorrhizal fungus based on the anatomy of their association with the host roots: ectomycorrhizae and endomycorrhizae.

Ectomycorrhizae typically grow in the intercellular spaces of the root cortex (outer layer or "skin") and form a thick mantle of tissue around the exterior of the root tip. Hyphae (fine, threadlike filaments) extend outward into the surrounding soil to gather water and nutrients. The network of intercellular filaments, the Hartig net, forms the exchange sites where the host exchanges carbohydrates for nutrients from the fungus. Ectomycorrhizae occur primarily on members of the Pinaceae, Betulaceae and Fagaceae families.

Endomycorrhizae grow mainly inside the cortical cells (*intra*cellular spaces). These don't form an external mantle so they are impossible to detect with the naked eye, but they do send out extensive hyphae into the surrounding soil.

Some endomycorrhizae form structures called vesicles and arbuscles within the root's cortical cells. These are known, naturally enough, as vesicular-arbuscular mycorrhizae, or VAM for short. This is the type of mycorrhiza we find on 90% of the world's higher plants. The arbuscles are tightly bunched hyphae that take carbohydrates from the host's cells, growing as they do so. Once they have completely filled the cells, they break down, releasing their nutrients to the host, and the fungus proceeds to colonize another cell. As for vesicles—nobody has yet discovered their function.

There is a subgroup called ectendomycorrhizae which, as you might have guessed, combines some of the features of the other two groups.

HOW DO MYCORRHIZAE GET THERE?

First, the potential fungal symbiont must produce viable mycelium (the fungal equivalent of roots) in the vicinity of the roots of the potential host. Usually this involves the germination of either spores or "resting" hyphae. This mycelium must then find its

The familiar (or should be) white micorrhizal mycelium on pine roots.

way to the roots of the host, which it does not do entirely by chance. The area of soil around a plant's roots (the rhizosphere) contains millions of minute organisms (microflora) that are influenced by the presence of the roots. By sensing this, the mycelium is able to navigate its way to the growing roots remarkably efficiently.

REPRODUCTION

VAM reproduce from chlamydospores, which are long-lived, thick-walled spores that are able to withstand the rigors of underground life until the roots of a potential host grow close by.

Ectomycorrhizae can reproduce either from spores, vegetatively from various types of clusters of hyphae, or from resting hyphae. In all cases, germination is stimulated by near proximity of roots of a potential host plant, via their effect on the microflora in the rhizosphere.

The benefits of mycorrhizae

Research continues into the benefits to plants of mycorrhizal associations and many have yet to be discovered. However, in the light of current knowledge, benefits can be divided into six categories.

WATER AND NUTRIENT UPTAKE

Mycorrhizae greatly increase the root's efficiency, largely because of the vastly increased absorptive surface area. The combined surface area of the millions of hyphae is far greater than that of non-mycorrhizal roots. In addition, the extending hyphae are able to draw on more distant, inaccessible supplies of water and nutrients than the roots can reach. Using radioactively labeled nutrients, scientists have shown that ectomycorrhizae are especially clever at absorbing phosphates and potassium, as well as alkali metals. VAM were shown to be efficient at absorbing phosphorus, copper, iron and calcium.

ALLEVIATION OF STRESS AND DISEASE

Environmental and cultural stresses influence plants'

susceptibility to and ability to combat bacterial diseases and are known to cause some nonbacterial maladies. VAM increase tolerance of environmental stresses (nutritional, drought, pathogens, soil toxicity, etc.) that predispose plants to disease. Increased uptake of nutrients, particularly micronutrients that are "locked" to soil particles and unavailable to the roots, makes the plant less vulnerable to plant pathogens, and more resistant to other environmental stresses such as cold and heat.

PROTECTIONS AGAINST ROOT PATHOGENS

Ectomycorrhizae, in particular, have recently been shown to resist attack by soil-borne pathogens. For example, there are several mycorrhizal fungi known to protect pines from pathogens such as *phytophthora*, *fusarium* and *rhizoctomia*. There are several mechanisms by which this occurs, many of which are thought to operate simultaneously.

- production of antibiotics by the fungus itself, which inhibit root pathogens
- the physical barrier created by the mantle of ectomycorrhizal hyphae
- production of chemical inhibitors by the host, induced by their reaction to invasion by the mycorrhizal fungus
- the establishment of populations of protective microbes in the rhizosphere.

ALTERED ROOT PHYSIOLOGY

Researchers have demonstrated that ectomycorrhizae produce growth hormones and regulators that are responsible for the altered metabolism and growth of the roots themselves. These substances enhance the ramification of root tips, the proliferation of roots, enlargement of cells and rooting of cuttings.

DETOXIFICATION OF SOILS

This is still a very sketchy area, as research is still in the early stages. However, scientists are now investigating what appears to be the capacity of mycorrhizae to assist plants to colonize soils that would otherwise be chemically toxic to them.

MAINTENANCE OF SOIL STRUCTURE

Mycorrhizae accelerate the decomposition of primary minerals and secrete organic "glue" (extracellular polysaccharides) that bonds the finer soil particles into larger, water-stable aggregates.

Significance of mycorrhizae in bonsai culture

If your bonsai is in a large enough pot with suitable soil and an adequate supply of water, nutrients and micronutrients, it's probably in reasonable health and growing well. But that doesn't necessarily mean it's performing to its full potential. One can get so accustomed to experiencing early autumns, weak second-growth flushes, midsummer shut-down, poor leaf condition in late summer and so on, that it becomes accepted as the norm. We're familiar with how mycorrhizae benefit pines, but let's see how they benefit bonsai in general by looking at the five points again.

WATER AND NUTRIENT UPTAKE
Newly repotted or collected trees don't have access to the entire growing medium simply because their roots don't fill the container. Mycorrhizal hyphae will extend from the existing roots throughout the container in a fraction of the time it would take non-mycorrhizal roots, thus utilizing all available moisture and nutrients. They also regulate the rate of nutrient uptake, thereby reducing the danger of "root burn." Later in the season, when the tree's water demand is higher, mycorrhizae can still help, even though the pot appears to be full of roots. Many soil ingredients, such as the harder grade of Akadama, calcined (baked) clay, pumice and even some bark chips, are impenetrable to roots. The hyphae, however, are able to penetrate the micropores in these particles and retrieve nutrients and micronutrients stored therein. In addition, they supply these to the tree in a form that the tree can use immediately.

ALLEVIATION OF STRESS AND DISEASE
Bonsai, by definition, are always under some form of stress (albeit controlled, hopefully) and this is made all the more significant with the increased usage of nonorganic, inert growing media and synthetic fertilizers. Therefore, bonsai are more susceptible to serious damage by disease and stress-related disorders than field-grown trees. Symptoms such as midsummer shut-down and early autumn, or discolored and tired foliage are all indications of stress or stress-related disease. In fact, if only one category of plant were crying out for the additional protection offered by mycorrhizae, it would be bonsai.

PROTECTIONS AGAINST ROOT PATHOGENS
Traditional bonsai wisdom states that if there's a problem with the tree's vigor, the cause is in the roots. Not all root pathogens are fatal—but more become fatal in a bonsai container than in the field, simply because of the slow rate of root growth and absence of the roots of other plants. Good tools, pots, soil and water hygiene, plus the choice of reputable organic fertilizers, should prevent most soil pathogens from entering the container. However, some are airborne and can arrive at any time, but many of these are unlikely to become a danger in a good bonsai soil. That still leaves the few that could become a danger. The added protection afforded by

mycorrhizae could give the bonsai grower the confidence to say that if there's a problem with the tree, it's probably *not* caused by the roots.

ALTERED ROOT PHYSIOLOGY
Increased ramification, increased root proliferation, enlargement of root cells (greater efficiency) and enhanced rooting of cuttings. Need more be said?

DETOXIFICATION OF SOILS
Once again, good soil and water hygiene should eliminate the possibility of accidental toxicity of bonsai soil. But there is some concern that calcined clays and other mineral soil ingredients can accumulate a toxic level of salts which could eventually harm the plant. If mycorrhizae can assist here, and it's not yet certain that they can, then better with than without!

MAINTENANCE OF SOIL STRUCTURE
As bonsai soil's organic matter—as well as its Akadama, loam or clay content—naturally breaks down into fine particles, they are rebonded by the mycorrhiza's polysaccharide secretion, thus maintaining an open, free-draining and well-aerated soil. You may have noticed how the soil in the pot of a pine with mycorrhizae is more friable and granular than that in the pot of a non-mycorrhizal pine.

Mycorrhiza inoculation
We all save some old mycorrhiza from our pines, and reintroduce it into the new soil when we repot. Does this work? Well, yes it does.

In fact there could well be enough spores, chlamydospores, sclerotia, rhizomorphs and resting hyphae left on the remaining roots to colonize the pot ten times over. But because you have pruned away the root tips, where the mycorrhiza forms, and your loose, granular soil has left you with an almost bare-rooted tree, you can never be sure, so reintroducing it is a very good idea. The same goes for other species with endomycorrhiza, which you can't see. Reintroducing chopped-up pieces of the pruned-away root tips will help to ensure recolonization of the pot.

However, there is one other important point. Remember we discovered that when the fragments or spores germinate, they are stimulated to do so by the microbial changes in the rhizosphere—which you don't have in your new soil and clean roots. The roots that the inoculated mycorrhiza is adhered to are now dead. One answer is to make sure that when you introduce the chopped-up mycorrhizal roots, they are in good close contact with living feeder roots. Another is to include a proportion of the previous soil in your new mix. Since the entire pot was probably completely filled with roots, practically all the soil would qualify as rhizosphere.

Is a tree ever old?

AGE AND THE AGING PROCESS

The irony of bonsai is that while the artist seeks to achieve the illusion of great age, the horticulturist seeks to maintain the vigor of a young tree.

ONE OF THE initial fascinations with bonsai is with their age. But just how important is the true age of a bonsai, and can the characteristics of true age be simulated?

In reply to an inquiry about the age of a particular tree, John Yoshio Naka commented: "But sir, you never ask a beautiful woman her age...."

This encapsulates the significance of age in bonsai—at least as far as aesthetics are concerned. Commercially, the older the customers think a bonsai is, the more they are likely to pay. In truth, it is how old or mature a bonsai *looks* that is important. If the design is intended to represent a 500-year-old pine, then the bonsai should have all the characteristics of a 500-year-old pine: fractured bark; fine, tight foliage; open branches with angular bends; and, of course, a domed (rather than pointed) crown.

Of course it helps a great deal if you can start with a plant that already has some or all of these characteristics. Old yamadori provide the quickest route, but they can have their drawbacks. As often as not, it is necessary to do heavy cutting and carving to reduce the size and to disguise the removal of heavy branches. This is extremely difficult to do convincingly. Once done badly it can't be rectified. Additionally, the new branches that are grown and trained by the artist are inevitably more juvenile in character, so the problem is still not entirely solved.

Natural aging

Trees don't age in the same linear way as animals. All animals transmute from infancy to senility in a strict chronological progression. Their physiological age—as marked by factors such as body shape, skin texture, hair color, etc.—and their "reproductive" age are precisely controlled by their chronological age according to a preordained timescale. Animals have, in a sense, only one growth phase that lasts from birth to natural death.

Trees, on the other hand, have separate chronological, physiological and what Dr. Peter Del Tredici of Harvard University's Arnold Arboretum explained to me as "ontogenetic" aging processes. The three phases of maturity develop independently, and at different rates in each individual tree, and even at different rates on different parts of the same tree.

For example, the chronologically oldest part of any plant is the cotyledal node, the section below where the first two "seed leaves" were borne. Ironically, this is also always the most juvenile part.

Conversely, if we take, as an example, a regularly flowering hawthorn, the flowering spurs are the newest (chronologically youngest) parts of the tree, but they are ontogenetically the oldest or most mature. As an array of twigs begins to flower, they transmute from ontogenetic juvenility to ontogenetic maturity. There will no longer be the annual flush of extension growth unless the mature sections are cut back to the juvenile buds at the base of the twigs. At the top of the same tree, however, there may well be areas where annual extension still occurs. In these juvenile areas there will be no flowers.

With some species the growth pattern is an indication of maturity—but not necessarily of age. Larch, cedar, hawthorn and ginkgo all have two types of shoot growth: vigorous extension shoots and short rosettes of foliage borne on spurs that only extend by a millimeter or less each year. Young seedlings have almost all extension growth; a sapling will have many rosettes but still produces vigorous annual extensions. An old tree will bear almost entirely spur growth.

However, when we talk of the appearance of age in bonsai terms, we are generally referring to the apparent evidence of physiological aging. These can be distilled into five characteristics:

- domed crown
- poise of the branches
- angular branch ramification
- distinct, separated foliage clouds
- and, of course, bark texture.

The first four are under the control of the artist or grower, but mature bark is something that comes only with time.

Mature, textured bark is arguably the most precious feature of almost any bonsai. With immature bark, few bonsai can appear mature. The exceptions are species such as many acers, taxus, fagus, etc., where the bark remains smooth throughout the tree's life. But most species produce a characteristic mature bark as they mature, usually adopting a plated or fissured texture. Others, such as *pseudocydonia* and *platanus*, have bark that flakes in patches to reveal many subtle shades of pink, green and buff. Betula and many *prunus* species allow their bark to peel in colorful layers.

How bark is formed

New layers of bark are formed annually in much the same way as the annual rings are formed beneath them. The single-cell-thick cambium layer produces new wood on the inside (the xylem) to conduct water and nutrients to the leaves, and new tissue on the outside (the phloem) to conduct sugars from the leaves to the rest of the tree. As each new layer of phloem is formed, the outermost dies and becomes bark.

The reasons why mature bark differs between species are complex and not yet fully understood. But in bonsai terms, we're more concerned with discovering how to accelerate its development.

Speed of growth is not the controlling factor. If a tree grows very rapidly, it can reach a considerable size and age but not display mature bark. The dying phloem remains elastic, and the stretching process associated with rapid trunk expansion retards the development of bark texture. There are two main influences on early bark maturation, one internal and one external.

Internally, it is the amount of phloem laid down annually in comparison with the trunk expansion that determines how quickly the bark will mature. A slowly expanding trunk with a heavy annual deposit of phloem will produce more bark. The bark becomes thick because it is not being stretched. The amount of phloem produced is governed by the amount of foliage; so a tree whose extension growth is retarded by external forces but which bears copious amounts of foliage will produce mature bark comparatively rapidly.

We can use this knowledge when we grow bonsai material in open ground. Allowing unfettered extension to thicken the trunk is only half the story. Once the trunk has more or less reached the desired thickness, be patient and let it stay in the ground a few more years. Feed heavily to build up as much weight of foliage as possible. Prune the long, vigorous leaders regularly to encourage even denser foliage. When you finally pot up, you'll have material that has mature bark character that would take decades to develop in a pot.

OLD BONSAI NEVER DIE...

Growing trees in small containers, where they are artificially dwarfed by their restricted roots and by continual injury, is undoubtedly stressful for them. Why is it, then, that they appear to live so long?

Well, in a sense the question is its own answer. Assuming a wild tree remains healthy, it eventually reaches its genetically predetermined height, whereupon the distance between the functioning root tips and the foliage is the maximum the tree's system can accommodate. No further extension is possible, so the tree begins to deteriorate. Structural degradation occurs, branches die and fall, and eventually the tree dies. However, in a bonsai container no tree ever reaches this stage.

We know that the wood in the center of the trunk of any tree is dead and is only necessary for structural strength—to hold the tree upright. The only living parts of the trunk and branches are the phloem, the cambium and the xylem. Neither the phloem nor the xylem are ever more than a few years old, and the cambium is constantly replenishing itself. So, in this sense, the living parts of a tree are only ever a few years old. Constant pruning of vegetative and root growth prevents the tree from reaching its full ontogenetic maturity—it is forever youthful and, in theory at least, should never die of old age.

Index